THE ULTIMATE

Hot and Spicy Cookbook

THE ULTIMATE

Hot and Spicy Cookbook

200
OF THE MOST FIERY,
MOUTH-SEARING AND PALATE-PLEASING
RECIPES EVER

LORENZ BOOKS
NEW YORK • LONDON • SYDNEY • BATH

This edition published in the UK in 1997 by Lorenz Books

This edition published in the USA by Lorenz Books
27 West 20th Street, New York, NY 10011

LORENZ BOOKS are available for bulk purchase for sales promotion and for
premium use. For details write or call the Manager of Special Sales,
Lorenz Books, 27 West 20th Street, New York, NY 10011; (212) 807-6739.

© 1997 Anness Publishing Limited

Lorenz Books is an imprint of Anness Publishing Limited

ISBN 1 85967 367 8

Publisher: Joanna Lorenz
Senior Cookery Editor: Linda Fraser
Project Editor: Anne Hildyard
Designer: Siân Keogh
Jacket Design and pages 1, 3, 6 & 7: Janet James
Jacket Illustration: Neil Packer
Book Illustrations: Madeleine David
Photography: William Adams-Lingwood, Karl Adamson, Edward Allwright,
David Armstrong, Steve Baxter, James Duncan, Nelson Hargreaves,
Amanda Heywood, Janine Hosegood, David Jordan, Patrick McLeavey,
Michael Michaels and Thomas Odulate
Recipes: Kit Chan, Jacqueline Clark, Roz Denny, Rafi Fernandez,
Christine France, Silvana Franco, Sarah Gates, Deh-Ta Hsiung, Shehzad Husain,
Elizabeth Ortiz Lambert, Sallie Morris, Hilaire Walden, Laura Washburn,
Pamela Westland, Steven Wheeler and Judy Williams
Food for Photography: Carla Capalbo, Kit Chan, Jacqueline Clark,
Joanne Craig, Rosamund Grant, Carole Handslip, Jane Hartshorn,
Wendy Lee, Lucy McKelvie, Annie Nichols, Jane Stevenson,
Steven Wheeler and Elizabeth Wolf-Cohen
Stylists: Hilary Guy, Clare Hunt, Maria Kelly, Patrick McLeavey, Blake Minton,
Thomas Odulate and Kirsty Rawlings

Printed and bound in Singapore

5 7 9 10 8 6 4

CONTENTS

Introduction 6

Spicy Soups *16*

Sizzling Appetizers and Snacks *36*

Fiery Fish and Seafood *64*

Scorching Meat and Poultry *96*

Hot and Vibrant Vegetables and Salads *132*

Flame-filled Rice and Noodles *166*

Searing-hot Side Dishes, Salsas and Relishes *202*

Sweet and Spicy Desserts and Cakes *222*

Spiced Drinks *244*

Index *254*

INTRODUCTION

IF VARIETY is the spice of life, it certainly must be said that spices give life – or at least food – its variety.

In all their idiosyncratic guises, spices lend richness, heat and complexity to literally every food imaginable, and it is impossible to conceive of a cuisine that does not benefit from unique and distinctive spicing. In fact, from the sun-drenched Caribbean to the deserts of the Middle East, the dense jungles of Vietnam and Indonesia, the bustling sidewalk stalls of Thailand, the great plains of Africa, the crowded streets of Mexico, and the spirited southwestern United States, "hot and spicy" defines good eating for millions of people who would not dream of consuming bland, unseasoned food when piquant delights are available at every turn.

Attention-grabbing spices are nothing if not highly particular, well-defined and capable of transforming dishes with a single pinch. For example, what would a searing Indian vindaloo taste like without its delicately balanced curry? Or a Thai Beef Salad without the powerful punch of chilies? Blackened Chicken Breasts without Cajun seasonings? Jerk Chicken without Habanero chili peppers? Probably like King Lear's meat without salt – in other words: not much. Indeed, for thousands of years, the right spice, or combination of spices, has actually helped define individual cultures by lending a nation's or a people's cuisine a flavor and a style that is unmistakably its own. Within these pages you will find an exhilarating, mind-expanding, and palate-tingling collection of recipes from every corner of the world.

Archaeological evidence shows that the cultivation of chili peppers thrived among the Aztecs of South America over 2000 years ago. Among Asian cultures, subtle and varied spicing has been prevalent for years. Some gastronomes hold that spicing first became popular in medieval Europe to enhance the keeping qualities and mask the taste and smell of food that had gone rancid in the days before refrigeration. Whatever their original use, spices became one of the most precious and desired commodities on the market – spices such as pepper and cinnamon from lands as far off as Sumatra and Ceylon were traded for land and even used to pay taxes (you'd probably be audited if you tried that today!).

What is certain is that whatever the origins of spices, we would live – and eat – in a dull world without them. Surely the sensual pleasure of a well-seasoned meal is reason enough to value the spices that make modern dining such an adventure.

With *The Ultimate Hot and Spicy Cookbook* in hand, mouth-searing, tongue-teasing meals will explode from your kitchen, energizing and inspiring all those who share with you the most exciting dishes around.

HOT AND SPICY INGREDIENTS

ALLSPICE

Available whole or ground, allspice are small, dark brown berries similar in size to large peppercorns. They can be used in sweet or savory dishes and have a flavor of nutmeg, cinnamon and clove, hence the name.

CARDAMOM

These pods are green, black and creamy-beige, green being the most common. Whole pods are used in rice and meat dishes to add flavor and should not be eaten. Black seeds are used in desserts.

CHILIES

Chilies are available from food stores and supermarkets. They are grown on a dwarf bush with small dense green leaves, white flowers and red or green finger shaped fruit. In general, the green chili is less hot and has a rather earthy heat; the red is usually hotter and is often very fiery.

To prepare chilies, remove the cap from the stalk end and slit it from top to bottom with a small knife. Under running water, scoop out the seeds with the knife point. The fire comes from the seeds so leave them if you like food to be fiercely hot. Chilies contain volatile oil that can irritate the skin and

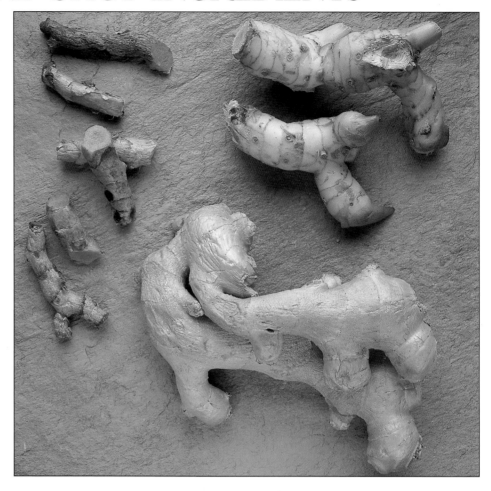

Clockwise from left: fresh turmeric roots before being ground to a fine powder, cut to show their vivid golden color, creamy colored fresh galangal roots, showing typical rings on the skin and pink nodules, and a large piece of unpeeled fresh root ginger showing the characteristic silvery brown skin.

sting the eyes, so it is best to use rubber gloves when preparing chilies, or wash hands afterwards with soap and water.

There are many different varieties of chilies. The small red and green fresh chilies are known as Thai or bird's eye chilies and are extremely hot. One of the hottest varieties is the fat and fiery Scotch Bonnet or *habanero*. It has a spicy smell and flavor and can be red, green, yellow or brown. There are innumerable types of chilies that are indigenous to Mexico. The most commonly used fresh green chilies are *serrano*, *jalapeño* and *poblano*. These varieties are all very hot.

Dried chilies are very popular and

In the spice chest (top right), from the left: cayenne pepper, fennel seeds and ground turmeric. On the table: fresh red and green chilies.
In the large bowl: a selection of ingredients for an Indian curry: red chilies, eggplants, okra, bitter gourds, bay leaves, red bell peppers; and in the small bowl: dried coriander seeds.

From left: fresh, glossy lime leaves, lemon grass and fresh cilantro leaves and root.

there are numerous varieties available. The most commonly used dried chilies are *ancho*, which is full-flavored and mild; *chipotle*, a very hot variety; *mulato*, which is pungent, and the hot *pasilla*.

CHILI PRODUCTS

Cayenne pepper is a pungent spicy powder made from a blend of small ripe red chilies.

Chili powder is made from dried, ground chilies and is often mixed with other spices and herbs.

Chili flakes are made from dried, crushed chilies and are used in pickles and sauces.

Chili oil is widely used in Chinese cooking. Dried red chilies are heated with vegetable oil to make this hot, pungent condiment.

Chili paste is a convenient way of adding fiery heat to sauces.

Hot pepper sauce is made from red chilies and vinegar and is used to sprinkle over many dishes.

CINNAMON

Available as bark or in the ground form, cinnamon has a woody aroma with a fragrant and warm flavor. The powdered form is widely used in the Middle East, especially in Khoresh.

Cinnamon is a versatile spice and is good in lamb dishes as well as in spiced drinks, fruit compotes, chocolate cakes and desserts.

CLOVES

Cloves are used in spice mixtures such as garam masala and in many meat and rice dishes. They can also be used to add spicy flavor to fruit and desserts.

CORIANDER

This spice is used throughout the world. It is available as either whole seeds or ground powder. The ripe seeds have a sweet, spicy aroma with a hint of orange flavor. Coriander can be used in both sweet and savory dishes and is one of the essential ingredients in curry powder. The flavor of coriander can be accentuated by dry-frying.

The leaves, known as cilantro, are essential in the cooking of South-East Asia and India and the root is often used in Thai cooking.

CUMIN

Cumin is available as small brown ridged seeds or in the ground form. Both types have a characteristic pungent, warm flavor. Cumin is also often dry-roasted to bring out the flavor. This spice is popular in the Middle East; it is used in spice mixtures such as garam masala and is added to pickles and salads. Cumin is one of the main ingredients of curry powder.

CURRY PASTE

Curry pastes are made by pounding together spices and red or green chilies. They are ferociously hot and will keep for about 1 month in the fridge.

FISH SAUCE

Known as *nam pla,* this is a commonly used flavoring in Thai dishes in the same way that soy sauce is used in Chinese cooking. Fish sauce is made from salted anchovies and it contributes pungent salty flavor to any dish.

Clockwise from top left: red chilies, mild, glossy green Kenyan chilies, hot green chilies, green chilies, orange Thai chilies, red birdseye chilies and green birdseye chilies.

Clockwise from top left: green jalapeño chilies, large green anaheim chilies, small green chilies, chipotle (smoked dried jalapeño chilies), dried mulato chilies, dried habanero chilies, dried pasilla chilies, green bell peppers, and (center top left) yellow and red Scotch Bonnet chilies, (center right) fresh red chilies.

FIVE-SPICE POWDER

This reddish brown powder is a combination of five ground spices – star anise seed, fennel, clove, cinnamon and Szechuan pepper. Used sparingly, it has a wonderful flavor, but it can be dominant if too much is added.

GALANGAL

This is a member of the ginger family and looks rather similar to fresh root ginger. The root is a creamy color, with a translucent skin that has rings, and may have pink nodules rather like young ginger. It has a refreshing sharp, lemony taste and is best used fresh, although it is available in dried or powder form. If you cannot find fresh galangal, use about 1 teaspoon of the dried powder to replace each inch of fresh galangal.

To prepare, cut a piece of the required size. Trim off any knobbly bits, then peel carefully, as the tough skin has an unpleasant taste. Slice to use in a paste and use up as soon as possible after peeling, to prevent loss of flavor. The flesh is much more woody and fibrous than ginger and has a distinctive, pine-like smell. Store galangal wrapped, in the salad drawer of the fridge.

GARAM MASALA

This spice mixture is made from a variety of spices and can be a simple blend, consisting of two or three spices and herbs, or a more complex masala, made from twelve or more different

Previous pages
Hot and Spicy ingredients from left to right, from top row:

Whole cloves, dried ground ginger, fresh root ginger and green cardamoms.

Tamarind pulp, whole cumin seeds, garam masala, saffron, garlic, bay leaves and fresh cilantro.

Whole black mustard seeds, ground cumin, whole nutmeg, black peppercorns, fennel seeds, whole cinnamon sticks and paprika.

Curry leaves, ground turmeric, fresh mint leaves, fenugreek seeds and ground coriander.

Curry powder, sesame seeds, chili powder, dried red chilies and coriander seeds.

Opposite page: A selection of spices, left to right from top row: paprika, whole green cardamoms, cumin seeds, saffron strands, ground turmeric, whole nutmeg and mace, ground sumac, cinnamon sticks and ground nutmeg.

spices. The dry spices and seeds are often dry-roasted first and sometimes whole spices are used. Garam masala may be added to the dish at different cooking stages.

GINGER

A root of Chinese and Indian origin with a silvery brown skin, ginger is best used fresh, and should be peeled and chopped or crushed before cooking. It is available in supermarkets – look for shiny fat roots that are not shriveled. Store in the salad drawer of the fridge, wrapped in kitchen paper. Chopped ginger is available in jars and keeps well in the fridge. Ginger makes a good alternative to galangal in Thai cooking.

LEMON GRASS

This tropical grass has a fresh, highly aromatic lemony taste and is a vital ingredient in South-East Asian cooking. It combines well with garlic and chilies and is pounded to a paste then added to curries. Unless it is finely chopped, lemon grass is usually removed before serving as it has a very fibrous texture.

LIME LEAVES

These glossy, dark green leaves come from the kaffir lime tree. They have a pleasing, distinctive smell and can be torn or left whole. Lime leaves can be frozen and used straight from the freezer in curries and sauces.

NUTMEG

Whole nutmegs are the hard aromatic seeds of an evergreen tree. The spice, which has a sweet, nutty flavor, is widely used all over the world. Whole nutmegs can be grated for cooking, but the ground spice is often used, particularly in the Middle East. Nutmeg can be used in both savory and sweet dishes.

PAPRIKA

This is made from a mixture of ground dried red peppers. Both mild and hot peppers are used, but paprika is always milder than cayenne pepper. It is used in the Middle East in soups, meat dishes, salad dressings and as a garnish.

PEPPERCORNS

White, green and black peppercorns are berries from the same plant, picked at different stages of maturity, and are used whole and ground. Pepper has a pungent flavor and can be used in either savory or sweet dishes. Peppercorns can be used whole, crushed or ground.

Szechuan pepper is also known as anise pepper or Chinese pepper. The berries are red-brown in color and are prickly. They have a spicy aroma and a strong, rather numbing taste.

SAFFRON

Made from the dried stamens of a type of crocus, saffron has a superb aroma and flavor. It also adds a delicate yellow color to food. For the best results it should be ground to a powder and diluted in a small amount of boiling water.

TAMARIND

An acidic-tasting tropical fruit that resembles a bean pod. It is added to curries to give a sharp flavor. Tamarind is usually sold dried or pulped. To make tamarind juice, soak a piece of tamarind pulp in warm water for about 10 minutes. Squeeze out as much tamarind juice as possible by pressing all the liquid through a sieve.

TURMERIC

Turmeric is another member of the ginger family. When the whole spice is peeled or scraped, a rich golden root is revealed. Turmeric adds a distinctive flavor and rich yellow color to meat and rice dishes. It is widely used throughout the Middle East and India. Because of its strong, bitter flavor, turmeric should be used sparingly.

ZERESHK

This is a small sour berry that comes from Iran. It is traditionally served with Persian rice dishes.

SPICY SOUPS

Soups are always satisfying and warming, and these soups certainly fill the bill. Drawn from Thailand, Africa, India and the Middle East, where chilies and spices are everyday foods, the recipes are a rich mixture of flavorful ingredients, enlivened by the addition of hot pickles, bell peppers and chilies, as well as aromatic spices. Hot and Spicy Seafood Soup and Mulligatawny Soup are sure to stimulate the appetite.

Tortilla Soup

INGREDIENTS

Serves 4–6

1 tablespoon vegetable oil
1 onion, chopped
1 large garlic clove, minced
2 tomatoes, peeled, seeded
   and chopped
½ teaspoon salt
10 cups chicken stock
1 carrot, diced
1 small zucchini, diced
1 skinless, boneless chicken breast half,
   cooked and shredded
6 canned green chilies, chopped

To garnish
4 corn tortillas
oil, for frying
1 small, ripe avocado
2 scallions, chopped
chopped fresh cilantro

1 Heat the oil in a saucepan. Add the onion and garlic and cook over medium heat for 5–8 minutes, until just softened. Add the tomatoes and salt and cook for 5 minutes more.

2 Stir in the chicken stock. Bring the liquid to a boil, covered, then lower the heat and simmer for about 15 minutes more.

3 Meanwhile, for the garnish, trim the tortillas into squares, then cut them into strips.

4 Put a ½-inch layer of oil in a frying pan and heat until hot but not smoking. Add the tortilla strips, in batches, and fry until just beginning to brown, turning occasionally. Remove with a slotted spoon and drain on paper towels.

5 Add the carrot to the soup. Cook, covered, for 10 minutes. Add the zucchini, chicken and chilies, and continue cooking, uncovered, for about 5 minutes, or until the vegetables are just tender.

6 Meanwhile, peel and pit the avocado. Chop into fine dice.

7 Divide the tortilla strips among four soup bowls and sprinkle each one with the avocado. Ladle in the soup, then sprinkle the scallions and cilantro on top. Serve immediately.

Tamarind Soup with Peanuts and Vegetables

Sayur Asam is a colorful and refreshing soup from Jakarta with more than a hint of sharpness.

INGREDIENTS

Serves 4 or 8 as part of a buffet
For the spice paste
5 shallots or 1 medium red
   onion, sliced
3 garlic cloves, crushed
1 inch *laos,* peeled and sliced
1–2 fresh red chilies, seeded and sliced
3 tablespoons raw peanuts
1 teaspoon shrimp paste
5 cups well-flavored chicken or
   vegetable broth
½ cup salted peanuts, lightly crushed
1–2 tablespoons dark brown sugar
1 teaspoon tamarind pulp, soaked in
   5 tablespoons warm water for
   15 minutes
salt

For the vegetables
1 chayote, thinly peeled, seeds
   removed, flesh finely sliced
4 ounces green beans, trimmed and
   finely sliced
⅓ cup corn kernels (optional)
handful green leaves, such as
   watercress, arugula or Chinese
   cabbage, finely shredded
1 fresh green chili, sliced, to garnish

2 Pour in some of the broth to moisten and then pour this mixture into a pan or wok, adding the rest of the broth. Cook for 15 minutes with the lightly crushed peanuts and sugar.

3 Strain the tamarind, discarding the seeds, and reserve the juice.

4 About 5 minutes before serving, add the chayote slices, beans and corn, if using, to the soup and cook fairly rapidly. At the last minute, add the greens or cabbage.

5 Add the tamarind juice and taste for seasoning. Serve, garnished with slices of green chili.

1 Prepare the spice paste by grinding the shallots or onion, garlic, *laos,* chilies, raw peanuts and shrimp paste to a paste in a food processor or with a mortar and pestle.

Pumpkin and Chili Soup

INGREDIENTS

Serves 4–6

2 garlic cloves, crushed
4 shallots, finely chopped
½ teaspoon shrimp paste
1 tablespoon dried shrimp, soaked for
   10 minutes and drained
1 lemongrass stalk, chopped
2 green chilies, seeded
2½ cups chicken stock
1 pound pumpkin, cut into ¾-inch
   thick chunks
2½ cups coconut cream
2 tablespoons fish sauce
1 teaspoon sugar
4 ounces small cooked
   shelled shrimp
salt and freshly ground black pepper
2 red chilies, seeded and finely
   sliced, and 10–12 basil leaves,
   to garnish

1 Grind the garlic, shallots, shrimp
paste, dried shrimp, lemongrass,
green chilies and salt into a paste.

2 In a large saucepan, bring the
chicken stock to a boil, add the
ground paste and stir to dissolve.

3 Add the pumpkin and simmer for
about 10–15 minutes, or until the
pumpkin is tender.

4 Stir in the coconut cream, then
bring back to a simmer. Add the
fish sauce, sugar and ground black
pepper to taste.

5 Add the shrimp and cook until
they are heated through. Serve
garnished with the sliced red chilies
and basil leaves.

————— COOK'S TIP —————

Shrimp paste is used here to give a
wonderful savory flavor.

Spicy Vegetable Soup

INGREDIENTS

Serves 4

½ red onion
6 ounces each, turnip, sweet potato and
  pumpkin
2 tablespoons butter or margarine
1 teaspoon dried marjoram
½ teaspoon ground ginger
¼ teaspoon ground cinnamon
1 tablespoon chopped scallions
4 cups rich vegetable stock
2 tablespoons sliced almonds
1 fresh chili, seeded and chopped
1 teaspoon sugar
½ cup coconut cream
salt and freshly ground black pepper
chopped fresh cilantro, to garnish
  (optional)

1 Finely chop the onion, then peel the turnip, sweet potato and pumpkin and chop into medium-size dice.

2 Melt the butter or margarine in a large nonstick saucepan. Fry the onion for 4–5 minutes. Add the diced vegetables and fry for 3–4 minutes.

3 Add the marjoram, ginger, cinnamon, scallions, salt and pepper. Fry over a low heat for about 10 minutes, stirring frequently.

4 Add the vegetable stock, sliced almonds, chopped chili and sugar and stir well to mix, then cover and simmer gently for 10–15 minutes or until the vegetables are just tender.

5 Add the coconut cream to the soup and stir to mix. Sprinkle with chopped cilantro, if liked, spoon into warmed bowls and serve.

Plantain Soup with Corn and Chili

INGREDIENTS

Serves 4

2 tablespoons butter or margarine
1 onion, finely chopped
1 garlic clove, crushed
10 ounces yellow plantains, peeled and
    sliced
1 large tomato, peeled and chopped
1 cup corn
1 teaspoon dried tarragon, crushed
3¾ cups vegetable or chicken stock
1 green chili, seeded and chopped
pinch of grated nutmeg
salt and freshly ground black pepper

1 Melt the butter or margarine in a saucepan over a moderate heat, add the onion and garlic and fry for a few minutes until the onion is soft.

2 Add the plantains, tomato and corn and cook for 5 minutes.

3 Add the tarragon, vegetable stock, chili and salt and pepper to taste and simmer for 10 minutes or until the plantain is tender. Stir in the nutmeg and serve at once.

Spicy Groundnut Soup

This soup is widely eaten in Africa. Groundnuts (or peanuts) are spiced with a mixture of fresh ginger and chili powder with herbs added for extra flavor. The amount of chili powder can be varied according to taste, add more for a fiery hot soup.

INGREDIENTS

Serves 4

3 tablespoons pure groundnut paste
    or peanut butter
6¼ cups stock or water
2 tablespoons tomato paste
1 onion, chopped
2 slices fresh ginger
¼ teaspoon dried thyme
1 bay leaf
salt and chili powder
8 ounces white yam, diced
10 small okras, trimmed (optional)

1 Place the groundnut paste or peanut butter in a bowl, add 1¼ cups of the stock or water and the tomato paste and blend together to make a smooth paste.

2 Spoon the nut mixture into a saucepan and add the onion, ginger, thyme, bay leaf, salt, chili and the remaining stock.

3 Heat gently until simmering, then cook for 1 hour, stirring from time to time to prevent the nut mixture sticking.

4 Add the white yam, cook for another 10 minutes, and then add the okra, if using, and simmer until both are tender. Serve immediately.

Beef and Turmeric Soup

The addition of turmeric and saffron colors this satisfying soup a deep, vibrant yellow. It is a popular dish in Iran.

INGREDIENTS

Serves 6

2 large onions
2 tablespoons oil
1 tablespoon ground turmeric
½ cup yellow split peas
5 cups water
8 ounces ground beef
1 cup rice
3 tablespoons each fresh chopped
  parsley, cilantro and chives
1 tablespoon butter
1 large garlic clove, finely chopped
4 tablespoons chopped mint
2–3 saffron strands dissolved in
  1 tablespoon boiling water (optional)
salt and freshly ground black pepper
yogurt and nan bread, to serve

1 Chop one of the onions, then heat the oil in a large saucepan and fry the onion until golden brown. Add the turmeric, split peas and water, bring to a boil, then reduce the heat and simmer for 20 minutes.

— COOK'S TIP —

Fresh spinach is also delicious in this soup. Add 2 ounces finely chopped spinach leaves to the soup with the parsley, cilantro and chives.

2 Grate the other onion into a bowl, add the ground beef and seasoning and mix well. Using your hands, form the mixture into small balls, about the size of walnuts. Carefully add to the pan and simmer for 10 minutes.

3 Add the rice, then stir in the parsley, cilantro, and chives and simmer for about 30 minutes, until the rice is tender, stirring frequently.

4 Melt the butter in a small pan and gently fry the garlic. Add the mint, stir briefly and sprinkle over the soup with the saffron, if using.

5 Spoon the soup into warmed serving dishes and serve with yogurt and nan bread.

Mulligatawny Soup

Mulligatawny (which means "pepper water") was introduced into England in the late eighteenth century by members of the army and colonial service returning home from India. It is a wonderfully spicy soup, that is best served with fresh bread.

INGREDIENTS

Serves 4

4 tablespoons butter or oil
2 large chicken pieces, about
    12 ounces each
1 onion, chopped
1 carrot, chopped
1 small turnip, chopped
about 1 tablespoon curry powder
4 cloves
6 black peppercorns, lightly crushed
¼ cup lentils
3¾ cups chicken stock
¼ cup golden raisins
salt and ground black pepper

1 Melt the butter or heat the oil in a large saucepan, then brown the chicken over a brisk heat. Transfer the chicken to a plate.

2 Add the chopped onion, carrot and turnip to the saucepan and cook, stirring occasionally, until they are lightly colored. Stir in the curry powder, cloves and black peppercorns and cook for 1–2 minutes more before adding the lentils.

3 Pour the stock into the pan, bring to a boil, then add the golden raisins and chicken and any juices from the plate. Cover and simmer gently for about 1¼ hours.

4 Remove the chicken from the pan and discard the skin and bones. Chop the flesh, return to the soup and reheat. Check the seasoning before serving the soup piping hot.

COOK'S TIP

Choose red split lentils for the best color, although either green or brown lentils could also be used.

Spicy Yogurt Soup

A beautifully smooth soup with a spicy taste that never fails to surprise the palate.

INGREDIENTS

Serves 4–6

1½ cups plain yogurt, beaten
4 tablespoons gram flour
½ teaspoon chili powder
½ teaspoon turmeric
salt, to taste
2–3 green chilies, finely chopped
4 tablespoons vegetable oil
4 whole dried red chilies
1 teaspoon cumin seeds
3–4 curry leaves
3 garlic cloves, minced
2-inch piece of fresh ginger, crushed
fresh cilantro leaves, chopped,
  to garnish

1 Mix together the plain yogurt, gram flour, chili powder, turmeric and salt and strain them into a saucepan. Add the finely chopped green chilies and cook gently for about 10 minutes, stirring occasionally. Be careful not to let the soup boil over as you cook it.

2 Heat the oil in a frying pan and fry the remaining spices, minced garlic and fresh ginger until the dried chilies turn black.

3 Pour the oil and the spices over the yogurt soup, cover the pan and let rest for 5 minutes off the heat. Mix well, then gently reheat for 5 minutes more. Serve hot, garnished with the cilantro leaves.

VARIATION

Sugar can be added to this soup to bring out the full flavor. For an extra creamy soup, use strained yogurt instead of plain yogurt. Also, adjust the amount of chilies according to how hot you want the soup to be.

Hot and Spicy Seafood Soup

For a special occasion, serve creamy rice noodles in a spicy coconut-flavored soup, topped with seafood. There is a fair amount of work involved in the preparation but you can make the soup base ahead.

INGREDIENTS

Serves 4

4 red chilies, seeded and
    coarsely chopped
1 onion, coarsely chopped
1 piece *blacan*, the size of a
    bouillon cube
1 lemon grass stalk, chopped
1 small piece fresh ginger,
    coarsely chopped
6 macadamia nuts or almonds
4 tablespoons vegetable oil
1 teaspoon paprika
1 teaspoon ground turmeric
2 cups broth or water
2¹/₂ cups coconut milk
fish sauce
12 jumbo shrimp, peeled and deveined
8 scallops
8 ounces prepared squid, cut into rings
12 ounces rice vermicelli, soaked in
    warm water until soft
salt and freshly ground black pepper
lime halves, to serve

For the garnish

¹/₄ cucumber, cut into matchsticks
2 red chilies, seeded and finely sliced
2 tablespoons mint leaves
2 tablespoons fried shallots or onions

1 In a blender or food processor, process the chilies, onion, shrimp paste, lemon grass, ginger and nuts, until smooth in texture.

2 Heat 3 tablespoons of the oil in a large saucepan. Add the chili paste, and fry for 6 minutes. Stir in the paprika and turmeric, and fry for about 2 minutes more.

3 Add the broth or water and the coconut milk to the pan. Bring to a boil, reduce the heat, and simmer gently for 15–20 minutes. Season to taste with fish sauce.

4 Season the seafood with salt and pepper. Heat the remaining oil in a frying pan, add the seafood, and fry quickly for 2–3 minutes until cooked.

5 Add the vermicelli to the soup, and heat through. Divide among individual serving bowls. Place the fried seafood on top, then garnish with the cucumber, chilies, mint and fried shallots or onions. Serve with the limes.

COOK'S TIP

Blacan is dried shrimp paste. It is sold in small blocks and you will find it in most oriental supermarkets.

Ginger, Chicken and Coconut Soup

This aromatic soup is rich with coconut milk and intensely flavored with galangal, lemongrass and kaffir lime leaves.

INGREDIENTS

Serves 4–6

3 cups unsweetened coconut milk
2 cups chicken stock
4 lemongrass stalks, bruised
    and chopped
1-inch piece galangal, thinly sliced
10 black peppercorns, crushed
10 kaffir lime leaves, torn
11 ounces boneless chicken, cut
    into thin strips
1½ cups button mushrooms
5 tablespoons canned baby corn
4 tablespoons lime juice
3 tablespoons fish sauce
2 red chilies, chopped, to garnish
chopped scallions, to garnish
cilantro leaves, to garnish

1 Bring the coconut milk and chicken stock to a boil. Add the lemongrass, galangal, peppercorns and half the kaffir lime leaves, reduce the heat and simmer gently for 10 minutes.

2 Strain the stock into a clean pan. Return to the heat, then add the chicken, button mushrooms and baby corn. Cook for about 5–7 minutes or until the chicken is cooked.

3 Stir in the lime juice, fish sauce to taste and the rest of the lime leaves. Serve hot, garnished with red chilies, scallions and cilantro.

Hot and Sour Shrimp Soup with Lemon Grass

This classic Thai seafood soup – *Tom Yam Goong* – is probably the most popular and well-known soup from Thailand.

INGREDIENTS

Serves 4–6

1 pound jumbo shrimp
4 cups chicken stock or water
3 lemongrass stalks
10 kaffir lime leaves, torn in half
8-ounce can straw mushrooms, drained
3 tablespoons fish sauce
¼ cup lime juice
2 tablespoons chopped scallion
1 tablespoon cilantro leaves
4 red chilies, seeded and chopped
2 scallions, finely chopped

1 Shell and devein the shrimp and set aside. Rinse the shrimp shells and place in a large saucepan with the stock or water and bring to a boil.

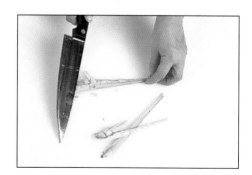

2 Bruise the lemongrass stalks with the blunt edge of a chopping knife and add them to the stock, together with half the lime leaves. Simmer gently for 5–6 minutes, until the stalks change color and the stock is fragrant.

3 Strain the stock and return to the saucepan and reheat. Add the mushrooms and shrimp, then cook until the shrimp turn pink.

4 Stir in the fish sauce, lime juice, scallions, cilantro, red chilies and the rest of the lime leaves. Taste and adjust the seasoning. It should be sour, salty, spicy and hot.

Spiced Lamb Soup

INGREDIENTS

Serves 4

4 ounces split black-eyed peas, soaked
   for 1–2 hours, or overnight

1½ pounds shoulder of lamb, cut into
   medium-size chunks

1 teaspoon chopped fresh thyme, or
   ½ teaspoon dried

2 bay leaves

5 cups stock or water

1 onion, sliced

8 ounces pumpkin, diced

2 black cardamom pods

1½ teaspoons ground turmeric

1 tablespoon chopped fresh cilantro

½ teaspoon caraway seeds

1 fresh green chili, seeded and chopped

2 green bananas

1 carrot

salt and freshly ground black pepper

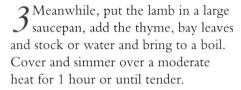

1 Drain the black-eyed peas, place
them in a saucepan and cover with
fresh cold water.

2 Bring the peas to a boil, boil
rapidly for 10 minutes and then
reduce the heat and simmer, covered,
for 40–50 minutes until tender, adding
more water if necessary. Remove from
the heat and set aside to cool.

3 Meanwhile, put the lamb in a large
saucepan, add the thyme, bay leaves
and stock or water and bring to a boil.
Cover and simmer over a moderate
heat for 1 hour or until tender.

4 Add the onion, pumpkin,
cardamom, turmeric, cilantro,
caraway, chili and seasoning and stir.
Bring back to a simmer and then cook,
uncovered, for 15 minutes or until the
pumpkin is tender, stirring occasionally.

5 When the peas are cool, spoon into a
blender or food processor with their
liquid and blend to a smooth purée.

6 Cut the bananas into medium slices
and the carrot into thin slices. Stir
into the soup with the peas and cook
for 10–12 minutes, until the vegetables
are tender. Adjust seasoning and serve.

Spicy Pepper Soup

This is a highly soothing broth for winter evenings, also known as Mulla-ga-tani. Serve with the whole spices, or strain and reheat if you like. The lemon juice may be adjusted to taste, but this dish should be distinctly sour.

INGREDIENTS

Serves 4–6

2 tablespoons vegetable oil
½ teaspoon freshly ground
    black pepper
1 teaspoon cumin seeds
½ teaspoon mustard seeds
¼ teaspoon asafoetida
2 whole dried red chilies
4–6 curry leaves
½ teaspoon turmeric
2 garlic cloves, crushed
1¼ cups tomato juice
juice of 2 lemons
½ cup water
salt, to taste
cilantro leaves, chopped, to garnish

— VARIATION —

If you prefer, use lime juice instead of lemon juice. Add 1 teaspoon tamarind paste for extra sourness.

1 In a large saucepan, heat the oil and fry the pepper, cumin and mustard seeds, asafoetida, red chilies, curry leaves, turmeric and garlic, until the chilies are nearly black and the garlic is golden brown.

2 Lower the heat and add the tomato juice, lemon juice, water and salt. Bring to a boil, then simmer the soup for about 10 minutes. Pour the soup into bowls, garnish with the chopped cilantro and serve.

Noodle Soup with Pork and Szechuan Pickle

INGREDIENTS

Serves 4

4 cups chicken broth
12 ounces egg noodles
1 tablespoon dried shrimp, soaked
  in water
2 tablespoons vegetable oil
8 ounces lean pork, finely shredded
1 tablespoon yellow bean paste
1 tablespoon soy sauce
4 ounces Szechuan hot pickle, rinsed,
  drained and shredded
pinch of sugar
salt and freshly ground black pepper
2 scallions, finely sliced, to garnish

1 Bring the broth to a boil in a large saucepan. Add the noodles, and cook until almost tender. Drain the dried shrimp, rinse under cold water, drain again, and add to the broth. Lower the heat, and simmer for about 2 minutes more. Keep hot. Heat the oil in a frying pan or wok. Add the pork, and stir-fry over a high heat for about 3 minutes.

2 Add the bean paste and soy sauce to the pork. Stir-fry for 1 minute more. Add the hot pickle with a pinch of sugar. Stir-fry for 1 minute more.

3 Divide the noodles and soup among individual serving bowls. Spoon the pork mixture on top, then sprinkle with the scallions. Serve the dish at once.

Snapper, Tomato and Tamarind Noodle Soup

Tamarind gives this light, fragrant noodle soup a slightly sour taste.

INGREDIENTS

Serves 4

8 cups water
2¹/₄ pounds red snapper (or other red
  fish such as bass)
1 onion, sliced
2 ounces tamarind pods
1 tablespoon fish sauce
1 tablespoon sugar
2 tablespoons vegetable oil
2 garlic cloves, finely chopped
2 lemon grass stalks, very
  finely chopped
4 ripe tomatoes, coarsely chopped
2 tablespoons yellow bean paste
8 ounces rice vermicelli, soaked in
  warm water until soft
4 ounces bean sprouts
8–10 basil or mint sprigs
¹/₄ cup roasted peanuts, ground
salt and freshly ground black pepper

1 Bring the water to a boil in a saucepan. Lower the heat, and add the fish and onion, with ¹/₂ teaspoon salt. Simmer gently until the fish is cooked right through.

2 Remove the fish from the stock, and set aside. Add the tamarind, fish sauce and sugar to the stock. Cook for 5 minutes, then strain the stock into a large pitcher or bowl. Carefully remove all of the bones from the fish, keeping the flesh in big pieces.

3 Heat the oil in a large frying pan. Add the garlic and lemon grass, and fry for a few seconds. Stir in the tomatoes and bean paste. Cook gently for 5–7 minutes, until the tomatoes are soft. Add the stock, bring back to a simmer, and adjust the seasoning.

4 Drain the vermicelli. Plunge it into a saucepan of boiling water for a few minutes, drain, and divide among individual serving bowls. Add the bean sprouts, fish, basil or mint, and sprinkle the ground peanuts on top. Fill each bowl with the hot soup.

Chicken Mulligatawny

INGREDIENTS

Serves 4–6

2-pound chicken, boned and skinned
2½ cups water
6 green cardamom pods
2-inch piece of cinnamon stick
4–6 curry leaves
1 tablespoon ground coriander
1 teaspoon ground cumin
½ teaspoon turmeric
3 garlic cloves, minced
12 whole peppercorns
4 cloves
1 onion, finely chopped
4 ounces coconut cream block
salt, to taste
juice of 2 lemons
deep-fried onions, to garnish
cilantro leaves, chopped, to garnish

1 Cut the chicken into pieces, then place it in a large saucepan with the water and cook until the chicken is tender. Skim the surface, then strain, reserving the stock and keeping the chicken pieces warm.

2 Return the chicken stock to the saucepan and reheat. Add the cardamom pods, cinnamon stick, curry leaves, coriander, cumin, turmeric, garlic, peppercorns, cloves, chopped onion, coconut cream, salt and lemon juice to the saucepan. Simmer for 10–15 minutes, then strain to remove the whole spices and return the chicken to the soup. Reheat the soup, garnish with deep-fried onions and chopped cilantro and serve.

— COOK'S TIP —

For a fast version of this soup, use pre-cooked chicken. Remove any skin and bone and chop into cubes. Add to the soup just before serving, then reheat.

Curried Noodle and Chicken Soup

Hot red curry paste, coconut milk, lime and red chilies are used to flavor this deliciously hot and spicy chicken soup, which originated in Burma.

INGREDIENTS

Serves 4–6

2½ cups unsweetened coconut milk
2 tablespoons red curry paste
1 teaspoon ground turmeric
1 pound chicken thighs, boned and cut
  into bite-size chunks
2½ cups chicken stock
4 tablespoons fish sauce
1 tablespoon dark soy sauce
juice of ½–1 lime
1 pound fresh egg noodles, blanched
  briefly in boiling water
salt and freshly ground black pepper

For the garnish
3 scallions, chopped
4 red chilies, chopped
4 shallots, chopped
4 tablespoons sliced pickled mustard
  greens, rinsed
2 tablespoons fried sliced garlic
cilantro leaves
4 fried noodle nests (optional)

1 In a large saucepan, add about one-third of the coconut milk and bring to a boil, stirring often with a wooden spoon until it separates.

2 Add the curry paste and ground turmeric, stir to mix completely and cook until fragrant.

3 Add the chicken and stir-fry for about 2 minutes, ensuring that all the chunks are coated with the paste.

4 Add the remaining coconut milk, chicken stock, fish sauce and soy sauce. Season with salt and freshly ground black pepper to taste. Simmer gently for 7–10 minutes. Remove from the heat and stir in the lime juice.

5 Reheat the noodles in boiling water, drain and divide between individual bowls. Divide the chicken between the bowls and ladle in the hot soup. Top each serving with a few of each of the garnishes.

SIZZLING APPETIZERS AND SNACKS

Appetizers and snacks offer lots of highly spiced, mouth-watering morsels and searingly hot bites. Spicy Kebabs set the taste buds tingling, while Samosas and Seafood Wontons with Spicy Dressing are perfect to hand round at a drinks party for a quick spicy appetizer. Start off a meal in lively style with Chilied Monkfish Packages.

Butterflied Shrimp in Chili Chocolate

Although the combination of hot and sweet flavors may seem odd, this is a delicious appetizer. Bitter chocolate adds richness without increasing the sweetness

INGREDIENTS

Serves 4

8 large raw shrimp, in the shell
1 tablespoon seasoned flour
1 tablespoon dry sherry
juice of 4 clementines or 1 large orange
½ ounce unsweetened, dark chocolate, chopped
2 tablespoons olive oil
2 garlic cloves, finely chopped
1-inch piece fresh ginger, finely chopped
1 small red chili, seeded and chopped
salt and freshly ground black pepper

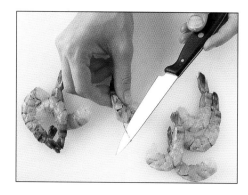

1 Peel the shrimp, leaving just the tail sections intact. Make a shallow cut down the back of each shrimp and carefully pull out and discard the dark intestinal tract. Turn over the shrimp so that the undersides are uppermost, then carefully split them open from tail to top, using a small, sharp knife, cutting almost, but not quite, to the back.

2 Press the shrimp down firmly to flatten them out. Coat with the seasoned flour and set aside.

3 Gently heat the sherry and clementine or orange juice in a small saucepan. When warm, remove from the heat and stir in the chopped chocolate until melted.

4 Heat the olive oil in a frying pan. Fry the garlic, ginger and chili over medium heat for 2 minutes until golden. Remove with a slotted spoon and reserve. Add the shrimp, cut side down, to the pan and cook for 2–3 minutes until golden brown with pink edges. Turn and cook for 2 minutes more.

5 Return the garlic mixture to the pan and pour over the chocolate sauce. Cook for 1 minute, turning the shrimp to coat them in the glossy sauce. Season to taste and serve hot.

Spicy Potatoes

Spicy potatoes, *patatas picantes,* are among the most popular tapas dishes in Spain, where they are sometimes described as *patatas bravas* (wild potatoes). There are many variations of this classic: boiled new potatoes or large wedges of fried potato may be used, but they are perhaps best simply roasted as in this recipe.

INGREDIENTS

Serves 2–4
8 ounces small new potatoes
1 tablespoon olive oil
1 teaspoon paprika
1 teaspoon chili powder
½ teaspoon ground cumin
½ teaspoon salt
Italian parsley, to garnish

1 Preheat the oven to 400°F. Prick the skin of each potato in two or three places with a fork, then place them in a bowl.

2 Add the olive oil, paprika, chili, cumin and salt, and toss well.

3 Transfer the potatoes to a roasting pan and bake for 40 minutes.

COOK'S TIP

This dish is delicious served with tomato sauce or Fiery Salsa – provide small forks for dipping.

4 Occasionally during cooking, remove the potatoes from the oven and turn them. Serve hot, garnished with Italian parsley.

Falafel

These tasty patties are one of the national dishes of Egypt. They can also be made with dried fava beans or chick-peas, and make an excellent appetizer.

INGREDIENTS

Serves 6
2½ cups dried white beans
2 red onions, chopped
2 large garlic cloves, crushed
3 tablespoons finely chopped
   fresh parsley
1 teaspoon ground coriander
1 teaspoon ground cumin
1½ teaspoons baking powder
oil, for deep frying
salt and freshly ground black pepper
tomato salad, to serve

1 Soak the white beans overnight in water. Remove the skins and process in a blender or food processor. Add the chopped onions, garlic, parsley, coriander, cumin, baking powder and seasoning and blend again to make a very smooth paste. Allow the mixture to stand at room temperature for at least 30 minutes.

2 Take walnut-sized pieces of mixture and flatten into small patties. Set aside again for about 15 minutes.

3 Heat the oil until it's very hot and then fry the patties in batches until golden brown. Drain on kitchen paper and then serve with a tomato salad.

Hummus

This popular Middle Eastern dip is widely available in supermarkets, but nothing compares with the delicious home-made variety.

INGREDIENTS

Serves 4–6
1 cup cooked chick-peas
½ cup tahini
3 garlic cloves
juice of 2 lemons
3–4 tablespoons water
salt and freshly ground black pepper
fresh radishes, to serve

For the garnish
1 tablespoon olive oil
1 tablespoon finely chopped
   fresh parsley
½ teaspoon cayenne pepper
4 black olives

1 Place the chick-peas, tahini, garlic, lemon juice, seasoning and a little of the water in a blender or food processor. Process until smooth, adding a little more water, if necessary.

2 Alternatively, if you don't have a blender or food processor, mix the ingredients together in a small bowl until smooth.

3 Spoon the mixture into a shallow dish. Make a dent in the middle and pour the olive oil into it. Garnish with parsley, paprika and olives and serve with the radishes.

COOK'S TIP

Canned chick-peas can be used for hummus. Drain and rinse under cold water before processing.

San Francisco Chicken Wings

INGREDIENTS

Serves 4

5 tablespoons soy sauce
1 tablespoon light brown sugar
1 tablespoon rice vinegar
2 tablespoons dry sherry
juice of 1 orange
2-inch strip of orange peel
1 star anise
1 teaspoon cornstarch
¼ cup water
1 tablespoon chopped fresh ginger
1 teaspoon chili-garlic sauce, to taste
3–3½ pounds chicken wings,
    tips removed

1 Preheat the oven to 400°F. Mix the soy sauce, sugar, vinegar, sherry, orange juice and peel, and anise in a saucepan. Bring to a boil.

2 Combine the cornstarch and water in a small bowl and stir until blended. Add to the boiling soy sauce mixture, stirring well. Boil for 1 minute more, stirring constantly.

3 Remove the soy sauce mixture from the heat and stir in the ginger and chili-garlic sauce.

4 Arrange the chicken wings, in one layer, in a large baking dish. Pour over the soy sauce mixture and stir to coat the wings evenly.

5 Bake in the center of the oven for 30–40 minutes, until the chicken wings are tender and browned, basting occasionally. Serve the chicken wings either hot or warm.

Cajun "Popcorn"

Cornmeal-coated spicy seafood resembles popcorn when made, hence the name for this tasty Cajun snack. Serve it with plenty of the deliciously creamy basil mayonnaise for a snack at any time of the day.

INGREDIENTS

Serves 8

2 pounds raw crayfish tails, peeled, or small shrimp, shelled and deveined
2 eggs
1 cup dry white wine
½ cup fine cornmeal (or all-purpose flour, if not available)
½ cup all-purpose flour
1 tablespoon snipped fresh chives
1 garlic clove, crushed
½ teaspoon fresh thyme leaves
¼ teaspoon salt
¼ teaspoon cayenne pepper
¼ teaspoon ground black pepper
oil, for deep-frying

For the mayonnaise

1 egg yolk
2 teaspoons Dijon mustard
1 tablespoon white wine vinegar
1 cup olive or vegetable oil
½ cup fresh basil leaves, chopped
salt and ground black pepper

1 Rinse the crayfish tails or shrimp in cold water. Drain well and set aside in a cool place.

2 Mix together the eggs and wine in a small bowl.

3 In a mixing bowl, combine the cornmeal and/or flour, chives, garlic, thyme, salt, cayenne and pepper. Gradually whisk in the egg mixture, blending well. Cover the batter and let stand for 1 hour at room temperature.

4 For the mayonnaise, combine the egg yolk, mustard and vinegar in a mixing bowl and add salt and pepper to taste. Add the oil in a thin stream, beating vigorously with a wire whisk. When the mixture is thick and smooth, stir in the basil. Cover and chill until ready to serve.

5 Heat 3 inches of oil in a large skillet or deep-fryer to a temperature of 350°F. Dip the seafood into the batter and fry in small batches for 2–3 minutes, until golden brown. Turn as necessary for even coloring. Remove with a slotted spoon and drain on paper towels. Serve hot, with the basil mayonnaise.

Mixed Tostadas

Like little edible plates, these golden crisp-fried tortillas can support any toppings that are not too juicy.

INGREDIENTS

Makes 14
oil, for shallow frying
14 freshly prepared unbaked corn tortillas
1 cup mashed red kidney or pinto beans
1 head iceberg lettuce, shredded
oil and vinegar dressing (optional)
2 cooked chicken breasts, skinned and thinly sliced
1 cup Guacamole (see Index)
1 cup coarsely grated Cheddar cheese
pickled *jalapeño* peppers, seeded and sliced, to taste

1 Heat the oil in a frying pan and fry the tortillas until golden brown on both sides and crisp but not hard.

2 Spread each tortilla with a layer of beans. Put a layer of shredded lettuce (which can be left plain or lightly tossed with a little dressing) over the beans.

3 Arrange pieces of chicken in a layer on top of the lettuce. Carefully spread over a layer of the guacamole and finally sprinkle over a layer of the grated cheese.

4 Arrange the mixed tostadas on a large platter. Serve on individual plates, but eat using your hands.

Quesadillas

These delicious filled and deep-fried tortilla turnovers make a popular snack, and smaller versions make excellent canapés.

INGREDIENTS

Makes 14
14 freshly prepared tortillas

For the filling
1 cup finely chopped or grated Cheddar cheese
3 *jalapeño* peppers, seeded and cut into strips
oil, for frying
salt

1 Have the tortillas ready, covered with a clean cloth. Combine the grated cheese and chili strips in a bowl. Season with salt. Set aside.

2 Heat the oil in a frying pan. Then, holding an unbaked tortilla on your palm, put a spoonful of filling along the center, avoiding the edges.

— COOK'S TIP —

For other stuffings, try leftover beans with chilies or chopped chorizo sausage fried with a little chopped onion.

3 Fold the tortilla and seal the edges by pressing or crimping together. Fry in hot oil, on both sides, until golden brown and crisp.

4 Using a spatula, lift out the quesadilla and drain it on paper towels. Transfer to a plate and keep warm while frying the remaining quesadillas. Serve hot.

Chilied Monkfish Packages

Hot red chili, garlic and lemon rind add tangy flavor to monkfish in these tasty little packages.

INGREDIENTS

Serves 4

1½ cups bread flour
2 eggs
4 ounces skinless monkfish fillet, diced
grated rind of 1 lemon
1 garlic clove, chopped
1 small red chili, seeded and sliced
3 tablespoons chopped fresh parsley
2 tablespoons light cream
salt and freshly ground black pepper

For the tomato oil

2 tomatoes, peeled, seeded and finely diced
3 tablespoons extra virgin olive oil
1 tablespoon fresh lemon juice

1 Place the flour, eggs and ½ teaspoon salt in a food processor, or blender; pulse until it forms a soft dough. Knead for 2–3 minutes. Wrap in plastic wrap and chill for 20 minutes.

2 Place the monkfish, lemon rind, garlic, chili and parsley in the clean food processor; process until very finely chopped. Add the cream, with plenty of salt and pepper, and process again to form a very thick paste.

3 Make the tomato oil by stirring the diced tomatoes with the olive oil and lemon juice in a bowl. Add salt to taste. Cover and chill.

4 Roll out the dough thinly on a lightly floured surface and cut out 32 rounds, using a 1½-inch plain cutter. Divide the filling among half the rounds, then cover with the remaining rounds. Pinch the edges tightly to seal, trying to exclude as much air as possible.

5 Bring a large saucepan of water to a simmer and poach the packages, in batches, for 2–3 minutes, or until they rise to the surface. Drain and serve hot, drizzled with the tomato oil.

Samosas

A selection of highly spiced vegetables in a pastry shell makes this delicious snack.

INGREDIENTS

Makes 30

1 package spring roll pastry, thawed and wrapped in a damp towel
vegetable oil, for deep-frying

For the filling

3 large potatoes, boiled and coarsely mashed
³/₄ cup frozen peas, boiled and drained
¹/₃ cup canned corn, drained
1 teaspoon ground coriander
1 teaspoon ground cumin
1 teaspoon amchur (dry mango powder)
1 small onion, finely chopped
2 green chilies, finely chopped
2 tablespoons cilantro leaves, chopped
2 tablespoons mint leaves, chopped
juice of 1 lemon
salt, to taste
chili sauce, to serve

1 Toss all the filling ingredients together in a large mixing bowl until they are all well blended. Adjust the seasoning with salt and lemon juice, if necessary.

2 Using one strip of pastry at a time, place 1 tablespoon of the filling mixture at one end of the strip and diagonally fold the pastry up to form a triangle shape.

3 Heat enough oil for deep-frying, and fry the samosas in small batches until they are golden brown. Keep them hot while frying the rest. Serve hot with chili sauce.

Guacamole

This popular Mexican dip can be served with tortilla chips, or used as a dip with fresh vegetables.

INGREDIENTS

Makes 2 cups

3 large, ripe avocados
3 scallions, minced
1 garlic clove, crushed
1 tablespoon olive oil
1 tablespoon sour cream
½ teaspoon salt
2 tablespoons fresh lemon juice
½ teaspoon cayenne pepper

1 Halve the avocados and remove the pits. Peel the halves. Put the avocado flesh in a large bowl.

2 With a fork, mash the avocado flesh coarsely.

3 Add the scallions, garlic, olive oil, sour cream, salt and lemon juice. Mash until well blended, but do not overwork the mixture. Small chunks of avocado should still remain. Adjust the seasoning, if necessary, with salt or lemon juice. Transfer the mixture to a serving bowl. Serve the dip immediately, sprinkled with the cayenne pepper.

> ─── COOK'S TIP ───
>
> Guacamole does not keep well, but if necessary, it can be stored in the fridge for a few hours. Cover the surface with plastic wrap to prevent discoloring.

Tomato Salsa

INGREDIENTS

Makes 3³/₄ cups

1 fresh hot green chili pepper, seeded and chopped
1 garlic clove
½ red onion, coarsely chopped
3 scallions, chopped
½ cup fresh cilantro leaves
1½ pounds ripe tomatoes, seeded and coarsely chopped
1–3 canned green chilies
1 tablespoon olive oil
2 tablespoons fresh lime or lemon juice
½ teaspoon salt, to taste
3 tablespoons tomato juice or water

1 In a food processor or blender, combine the fresh green chili, garlic clove, chopped red onion, scallions and fresh cilantro leaves. Process together until everything is finely chopped.

2 Add the tomatoes, canned chilies, olive oil, lime or lemon juice, salt and tomato juice or water. Pulse on and off until chopped; the tomato salsa should be chunky.

3 Transfer to a bowl and taste for seasoning. Let stand for at least 30 minutes before serving. This salsa is best served the day it is made.

> ─── COOK'S TIP ───
>
> For less heat, remove the seeds from both fresh and canned chilies.

Seafood Wontons with Spicy Dressing

These tasty shrimp and crabmeat wontons are spiced with chili and ginger, and served with a spicy sauce.

INGREDIENTS

Serves 4

8 ounces raw shrimp, peeled
   and deveined
4 ounces white crabmeat, picked over
4 canned water chestnuts, finely diced
1 scallion, finely chopped
1 small green chili, seeded and
   finely chopped
½ teaspoon grated fresh ginger
20−24 wonton wrappers
1 egg, separated
salt and freshly ground black pepper
cilantro leaves, to garnish

For the spicy dressing

2 tablespoons rice vinegar
1 tablespoon chopped pickled ginger
6 tablespoons olive oil
1 tablespoon soy sauce
3 tablespoons chopped cilantro
2 tablespoons diced red bell pepper

1 Finely dice the shrimp, and place in a bowl. Add the crabmeat, water chestnuts, scallion, chili, ginger and egg white. Season with salt and pepper, and stir well.

2 Place a wonton wrapper on a board. Put about 1 teaspoon of the filling just above the center of the wrapper. With a pastry brush, moisten the edges of the wrapper with a little of the egg yolk. Bring the bottom of the wrapper up over the filling. Press gently to expel any air, then seal the wrapper neatly in a triangle.

3 For a more elaborate shape, bring the two side points up over the filling, overlap the points, and pinch the ends firmly together. Place the filled wontons on a large baking sheet, lined with wax paper, so that they do not stick together.

4 Half fill a large saucepan with water. Bring to simmering point. Add the filled wontons, a few at a time, and simmer for 2−3 minutes. The wontons will float to the surface. When ready, the wrappers will be translucent and the filling should be cooked. Remove the wontons with a large slotted spoon, drain them briefly, then spread them on trays. Keep warm while cooking the remaining wontons.

5 Make the cilantro dressing by whisking all the ingredients together in a bowl. Divide the wontons among serving dishes, drizzle with the dressing, and serve garnished with a handful of cilantro leaves.

Deviled Kidneys

"Deviled" dishes are always hot and spicy. If you have time, mix the spicy ingredients together in advance to give the flavors time to mingle and mature.

INGREDIENTS

Serves 4

2 teaspoons Worcestershire sauce
1 tablespoon prepared English mustard
1 tablespoon lemon juice
1 tablespoon tomato paste
pinch of cayenne pepper
3 tablespoons butter
1 shallot, finely chopped
8 lamb's kidneys, skinned, halved and cored
salt and ground black pepper
1 tablespoon chopped fresh parsley, to garnish

1 Mix the Worcestershire sauce, mustard, lemon juice, tomato paste, cayenne pepper and salt together to make a sauce.

2 Melt the butter in a frying pan, add the chopped shallot and cook, stirring occasionally, until it is softened but not colored.

3 Stir the kidney halves into the shallot in the pan and cook over medium-high heat for about 3 minutes on each side.

4 Pour the sauce over the kidneys and quickly stir so that they become evenly coated. Serve the dish immediately, sprinkled with fresh chopped parsley.

COOK'S TIP

To remove the cores from the lamb's kidneys, use sharp kitchen scissors, rather than a knife – you will find that it is much easier to do so.

Desert Nachos

Tortilla chips are livened up with jalapeños in this quick-and-easy snack. Served with a variety of spicy Mexican dips, this always proves to be a popular dish.

INGREDIENTS

Serves 2

1 pound blue corn tortilla chips or
    ordinary tortilla chips
3 tablespoons chopped pickled
    jalapeños, according to taste
12 black olives, sliced
2 cups grated Cheddar cheese

To serve

guacamole
tomato salsa
sour cream

1 Preheat the oven to 350°F. Put the tortilla chips in a 9 x 13-inch baking dish and spread them out evenly. Sprinkle the jalapeños, black olives and grated cheese evenly over the tortilla chips.

2 Place the prepared tortilla chips in the top of the oven, and bake for 10–15 minutes until the cheese melts. Serve the nachos at once, with the guacamole, tomato salsa and sour cream for dipping.

Huevos Rancheros

INGREDIENTS

Serves 4

1-pound can refried beans
1¼ cups enchilada sauce
oil, for frying
4 corn tortillas
4 eggs
1¼ cups grated Cheddar cheese
salt and ground black pepper

1 Heat the refried beans in a saucepan. Cover and set aside.

2 Heat the enchilada sauce in a small saucepan. Cover and set aside.

COOK'S TIP

For a simple enchilada sauce, blend a can of tomatoes with 3 garlic cloves, 1 chopped onion, 3 tablespoons chili powder, 1 teaspoon each cayenne and cumin, and ½ teaspoon each dried oregano and salt.

3 Preheat the oven to 225°F. Put a ¼-inch layer of oil in a small nonstick frying pan, and heat it carefully. When the oil is hot, add the tortillas, one at a time, and fry for about 30 seconds on each side, until just crisp. Remove and drain the tortillas on paper towels. Keep them warm on a baking sheet in the oven. Discard the oil used for frying. Let the frying pan cool slightly, then wipe it with paper towels to remove all but a film of oil.

4 Heat the frying pan over low heat. Break in two eggs and cook until the whites are just set. Season with salt and pepper, then transfer to the oven to keep warm. Repeat to cook the remaining eggs.

5 To serve, place a tortilla on each of four plates. Spread a layer of refried beans over each tortilla, then top each with an egg. Spoon over the warm enchilada sauce, then sprinkle with the cheese. Serve hot.

Spicy Meat-filled Packages

In Indonesia the finest gossamer dough is made for *Martabak*. You can achieve equally good results using ready-made filo pastry or spring roll wrappers.

INGREDIENTS

Makes 16

1 pound lean ground beef
2 small onions, finely chopped
2 small leeks, very
    finely chopped
2 garlic cloves, crushed
2 teaspoons coriander seeds, dry-fried
    and ground
1 teaspoon cumin seeds, dry-fried
    and ground
1–2 teaspoons mild curry powder
2 eggs, beaten
1-pound package filo pastry
3–4 tablespoons sunflower oil
salt and freshly ground black pepper
light soy sauce, to serve

1 To make the filling, mix the meat with the onions, leeks, garlic, coriander, cumin, curry powder and seasoning. Turn into a heated wok, without oil, and stir constantly, until the meat has changed color and looks cooked, about 5 minutes.

2 Allow to cool and then mix in enough beaten egg to bind to a soft consistency. Any leftover egg can be used to seal the edges of the dough; otherwise, use milk.

3 Brush a sheet of filo with oil and lay another sheet on top. Cut the sheets in half. Place a large spoonful of the filling on each double piece of filo. Fold the sides to the middle so that the edges just overlap. Brush these edges with either beaten egg or milk and fold the other two sides to the middle in the same way, so that you now have a square package. Make sure that the package is as flat as possible, to speed cooking. Repeat with the other fifteen packages and place on a floured sheet of wax paper on a tray in the fridge.

4 Heat the remaining oil in a shallow pan and cook several packages at a time, depending on the size of the pan. Cook for 3 minutes on the first side and then turn them over and cook for another 2 minutes, or until heated through. Cook the remaining packages in the same way and serve hot, sprinkled with light soy sauce.

5 If preferred, these spicy packages can be cooked in a hot oven at 400°F for 20 minutes. Glaze with more beaten egg before baking for a rich, golden color.

Welsh Rabbit

This delicious supper dish is made from toast and a flavorful cheese sauce spiked with hot mustard and Worcestershire sauce. It doesn't, as the name might suggest, contain any meat. It is also called "Welsh Rarebit," although "rabbit" seems to have been the original name.

INGREDIENTS

Serves 4

4 thick slices of bread, crusts removed
2 tablespoons butter
2 cups grated aged Cheddar cheese
1 teaspoon English mustard powder
few drops Worcestershire sauce
4 tablespoons brown ale, beer or milk

COOK'S TIP

Use a strong-tasting cheese so the topping has plenty of flavor.

1 Preheat the broiler. Toast the bread on both sides until golden, then arrange in a single layer in a wide, shallow baking dish. Keep the toasted bread warm.

2 Slowly melt the butter in a small to medium, heavy-bottomed, preferably nonstick saucepan over very low heat, or in a bowl placed over a saucepan of hot water. Stir it constantly as it melts, then remove from the heat.

3 Stir the cheese, mustard powder and Worcestershire sauce into the melted butter, then slowly pour in the ale, beer or milk in a steady stream, stirring the cheese mixture all the time until very well blended.

4 Preheat the broiler. Spoon the Cheddar cheese mixture onto the toast in the baking dish, then place it under the hot broiler until it is bubbling hot and golden brown in color. Serve immediately.

Chicken Naan Pockets

This quick-and-easy dish is ideal for a snack lunch or supper.

INGREDIENTS

Serves 4

4 naan
3 tablespoons plain yogurt
1½ teaspoons garam masala
1 teaspoon chili powder
1 teaspoon salt
3 tablespoons lemon juice
1 tablespoon chopped fresh cilantro
1 fresh green chili, chopped
3¼ cups chicken, skinned, boned
   and cubed
1 tablespoon vegetable oil
8 onion rings
2 tomatoes, quartered
½ white cabbage, shredded
lemon wedges, 2 small tomatoes,
   halved, mixed salad leaves and fresh
   cilantro, to garnish

1 Using a small, sharp knife, carefully cut into the middle of each naan to make a pocket, then set them aside until needed.

2 In a medium mixing bowl, combine the plain yogurt, garam masala, chili powder, salt, lemon juice, fresh cilantro and chopped fresh green chili. Mix well. Pour this marinade over the chicken pieces and let marinate for about 1 hour.

3 After 1 hour preheat the broiler to very hot, then lower the heat to medium. Place the marinated chicken pieces in a flameproof casserole and broil for about 15–20 minutes, until they are tender and cooked through, turning the chicken pieces at least twice. Baste with the vegetable oil occasionally while cooking.

4 Remove the dish from the heat and fill each naan with the chicken and then with the onion rings, tomatoes and shredded cabbage. Serve garnished with lemon, tomatoes, salad leaves and cilantro.

Chicken Tikka

A mixture of ginger, garlic and chili powder adds a characteristic spicy taste to this popular Indian appetizer that is both quick and easy to cook.

INGREDIENTS

Serves 6

3¼ cups chicken, skinned, boned
   and cubed
1 teaspoon ginger pulp
1 teaspoon garlic pulp
1 teaspoon chili powder
¼ teaspoon turmeric
1 teaspoon salt
⅔ cup plain yogurt
4 tablespoons lemon juice
1 tablespoon chopped fresh cilantro
1 tablespoon vegetable oil
1 small onion, cut into rings, lime
   wedges, mixed salad and fresh
   cilantro, to garnish

1 In a medium mixing bowl, combine the chicken pieces, ginger and garlic pulp, chili powder, turmeric, salt, plain yogurt, lemon juice and fresh cilantro and let marinate for at least 2 hours.

2 Place the marinated chicken on a broiler tray or in a flameproof dish lined with foil, and baste with the vegetable oil.

3 Preheat the broiler to medium. Broil the chicken for about 15–20 minutes until cooked, turning and basting 2–3 times. Serve garnished with onion, lime, salad and cilantro.

—— COOK'S TIP ——

Chicken Tikka can be served with naan or chapatis, pickles and salad as a main dish for four people.

Spicy Kebabs

INGREDIENTS

Makes 18–20 balls

1 pound ground beef
1 egg
3 garlic cloves, crushed
½ onion, finely chopped
½ teaspoon freshly ground black pepper
1½ teaspoons ground cumin
1½ teaspoons dhania (ground coriander)
1 teaspoon ground ginger
2 teaspoons garam masala
1 tablespoon lemon juice
1–1½ cups fresh white bread crumbs
1 small chili, seeded and chopped
salt
oil, for deep frying
Kachumbali or spicy dip, to serve

1 Place the ground beef in a large bowl and add the egg, garlic, onion, spices, seasoning, lemon juice, about 1 cup of the bread crumbs and the chili.

2 Using your hands or a wooden spoon, mix the ingredients together until the mixture is firm. If it feels sticky, add more of the bread crumbs and mix again until firm.

3 Heat the oil in a large heavy pan or deep-fat fryer. Shape the mixture into balls or fingers and fry, a few at a time, for 5 minutes or until well browned all over.

4 Using a slotted spoon, drain the kebabs and then transfer to a plate lined with paper towels. Cook the remaining kebabs in the same way and then serve, if you like, with Kachumbali or a spicy dip.

Cod with Chili and Mustard Seeds

INGREDIENTS

Serves 4

2 tablespoons olive oil
1 teaspoon mustard seeds
1 large potato, cubed
2 slices of serrano ham, shredded
1 onion, thinly sliced
2 garlic cloves, thinly sliced
1 red chili, seeded and sliced
4 ounces skinless, boneless cod, cubed
½ cup vegetable stock
½ cup grated tasty cheese, such as
   Manchego or Cheddar
salt and freshly ground black pepper

COOK'S TIP

For a crisp topping, substitute half the
cheese with whole-wheat bread crumbs.

1 Heat the oil in a heavy-bottomed frying pan. Add the mustard seeds. Cook for a minute or two until the seeds begin to pop and splutter, then add the potato, ham and onion.

2 Cook, stirring regularly for about 10–15 minutes, until the potatoes are brown and almost tender.

3 Add the garlic and chili, and cook for 2 minutes more.

4 Stir in the cod cubes and cook for 2–3 minutes until white, then add the stock and plenty of salt and pepper. Cover the pan and cook for 5 minutes, until the fish is just cooked and the potatoes are tender.

5 Transfer the mixture to a casserole. Sprinkle over the grated cheese and place under a hot broiler for about 2–3 minutes until the cheese is golden and bubbling.

Fried Dough Balls with Fiery Salsa

These crunchy dough balls are accompanied by a hot and spicy tomato salsa. Serve them with a juicy tomato salad, if you prefer.

INGREDIENTS

Serves 10

4 cups white bread flour
1 teaspoon fast-rising dried yeast
1 teaspoon salt
2 tablespoons chopped fresh parsley
2 garlic cloves, finely chopped
2 tablespoons olive oil, plus extra
   for greasing
vegetable oil, for frying

For the salsa

6 hot red chilies, seeded and
   coarsely chopped
1 onion, coarsely chopped
2 garlic cloves, quartered
1-inch piece fresh ginger,
   coarsely chopped
1 pound tomatoes, coarsely chopped
2 tablespoons olive oil
pinch of sugar
salt and freshly ground black pepper

1 Sift the flour into a large bowl. Stir in the yeast and salt and make a well in the center. Add the parsley, garlic, olive oil and enough warm water to make a firm dough.

2 Gather the dough in the bowl together, then turn out onto a lightly floured surface or board. Knead for about 10 minutes, until the dough feels very smooth and elastic.

3 Rub a little oil into the surface of the dough. Return it to the clean bowl, cover with plastic wrap or a clean dish towel and let rise in a warm place for about 1 hour, or until doubled in bulk.

4 Meanwhile, make the salsa. Combine the chilies, onion, garlic and ginger in a food processor or blender and process together until very finely chopped. Add the tomatoes and olive oil, and process until smooth.

5 Strain the mixture into a saucepan. Add sugar, salt and pepper to taste and simmer gently for 15 minutes. Do not allow the salsa to boil.

6 Roll the dough into about 40 balls. Shallow fry in batches in hot oil for 4–5 minutes until crisp and golden. Drain on paper towels and serve hot, with the fiery salsa in a separate bowl for dipping.

COOK'S TIP

These dough balls can be deep-fried for 3–4 minutes or baked at 400°F for 15–20 minutes.

Cheese Fritters

These crisp fritters owe their inspiration to Italy. A note of caution – do be careful not to burn your mouth when you take your first bite, as the soft, rich cheese filling will be very hot.

INGREDIENTS

Makes 15–16
½ cup ricotta cheese
½ cup grated fontina cheese
⅓ cup finely grated Parmesan cheese
½ teaspoon cayenne pepper
1 egg, beaten, plus a little extra to seal the wontons
15–16 wonton wrappers
  oil for deep frying

1 Line a large baking sheet with wax paper, or sprinkle it lightly with flour. Set aside. Combine the cheeses in a bowl, then add the cayenne and beaten egg. Mix well.

2 Place one wonton wrapper at a time on a board. Brush the edges with egg. Spoon a little filling in the center. Pull the top corner down to the bottom corner, to make a triangle.

3 Transfer the filled wontons to the prepared baking sheet.

4 Heat the oil in a deep-fryer or large saucepan. Slip in as many wontons at one time as can be accommodated without overcrowding. Fry them for 2–3 minutes on each side, or until the fritters are golden. Remove with a slotted spoon. Drain on paper towels, and serve at once.

Chilled Soba Noodles with Nori

INGREDIENTS

Serves 4
12 ounces dried soba noodles
1 sheet nori seaweed

For the dipping sauce
1¼ cups fish broth
½ cup dark soy sauce
4 tablespoons mirin
1 teaspoon sugar
1 tablespoon fish sauce

Flavorings
4 scallions, finely chopped
2 tablespoons grated daikon
wasabi paste
4 egg yolks (optional)

COOK'S TIP

Daikon is a slim, white vegetable, sometimes also known as mooli.

1 Make the dipping sauce. Combine the broth, soy sauce, mirin and sugar in a saucepan. Bring rapidly to a boil, add the fish sauce, then remove from the heat. When cool, strain the sauce into a bowl and cover. This can be done in advance and the sauce kept chilled for up to a week.

2 Cook the soba noodles in a saucepan of lightly salted boiling water for 6–7 minutes or until just tender, following the manufacturer's directions on the package.

3 Drain and rinse the noodles under cold running water, shaking them gently to remove the excess starch. Drain well.

4 Toast the nori over a high gas flame or under a hot broiler, then crumble into thin strips. Divide the noodles among four serving dishes, and top with the nori. Serve each portion with an individual bowl of dipping sauce. Offer the flavorings separately.

FIERY FISH AND SEAFOOD

Fresh fish is popular all over the world and there are hundreds of ways of adding spicy flavor; fish can be fired up with hot red chilies or chili paste, pickled with jalapeño chilies or made into a curry with aromatic warm spices and spiked with hot chili powder. Steamed Fish with Chili Sauce is a delicious dish — the fish is cooked to perfection, with all the moistness and flavor retained.

Steamed Fish with Chili Sauce

In this red-hot dish from Thailand, whole fish is cooked with red chilies, ginger and lemon grass, then served with a mouth-tingling chili sauce.

INGREDIENTS

Serves 4

1 large or 2 medium firm fish, such as bass or grouper, scaled and cleaned
1 banana leaf or aluminum foil
2 tablespoons rice wine
3 red chilies, seeded and finely sliced
2 garlic cloves, finely chopped
³/₄-inch piece fresh ginger, finely shredded
2 lemongrass stalks, crushed and finely chopped
2 scallions, chopped
2 tablespoons fish sauce
juice of 1 lime

For the chili sauce

10 red chilies, seeded and chopped
4 garlic cloves, chopped
4 tablespoons fish sauce
1 tablespoon sugar
5 tablespoons lime juice

1 Rinse the fish under cold running water. Pat dry with paper towels. With a sharp knife, slash the skin of the fish a few times on both sides.

2 Place the fish on a banana leaf or piece of foil. Mix all the other ingredients and spread over the fish.

3 Place a small upturned plate or rack in the bottom of a wok and add about 2 inches boiling water. Lift the banana leaf, together with the fish, and place on the plate or rack. Cover with a lid and steam for about 10–15 minutes, or until the fish is cooked.

4 Place all the chili sauce ingredients in a food processor and process until smooth. You may need to add a little cold water.

5 Serve the fish hot, on the banana leaf if you like, with the sweet chili sauce to spoon over the top.

Fried Catfish Fillets with Piquant Sauce

Spicy fillets of catfish are fried in a herby batter and served with a wonderfully tasty sauce to create this excellent supper dish.

INGREDIENTS

Serves 4

1 egg
1/4 cup olive oil
squeeze of lemon juice
1/2 teaspoon chopped fresh dill
    or parsley
4 catfish fillets
1/2 cup flour
2 tablespoons butter or margarine
salt and ground black pepper

For the sauce

1 egg yolk
2 tablespoons Dijon mustard
2 tablespoons white wine vinegar
2 teaspoons paprika
1 1/4 cups olive or vegetable oil
2 tablespoons prepared horseradish
1/2 teaspoon chopped garlic
1 celery stalk, chopped
2 tablespoons tomato ketchup
1/2 teaspoon ground black pepper
1/2 teaspoon salt

1 For the sauce, combine the egg yolk, mustard, vinegar, and paprika in a mixing bowl. Add the oil in a thin stream, beating vigorously with a wire whisk to blend it in.

2 When the mixture is smooth and thick, beat in all the other sauce ingredients. Cover and chill until ready to serve.

3 Combine the egg, 1 tablespoon olive oil, the lemon juice, herbs and a little salt and pepper in a shallow dish. Beat until well combined.

4 Dip both sides of each catfish fillet in the egg and herb mixture, then coat lightly with flour, shaking off any excess from it.

5 Heat the butter or margarine with the remaining olive oil in a large heavy-bottomed frying pan. Add the fish fillets and fry until they are golden brown on both sides and cooked, for about 8–10 minutes. To test they are done, insert the point of a sharp knife into the fish: the flesh should be opaque in the center.

6 Serve the fried catfish fillets hot, accompanied by the piquant sauce in a dish.

— COOK'S TIP —

If you can't find catfish, use any firm fish fillets instead. Cod or haddock fillets would both make good substitutes.

Pickled Fish (Pescado en Escabeche)

INGREDIENTS

Serves 4

2 pounds whitefish fillets
4 tablespoons freshly squeezed lime or
　　lemon juice
1¼ cups olive or corn oil
2 whole cloves
6 peppercorns
2 garlic cloves
½ teaspoon ground cumin
½ teaspoon dried oregano
2 bay leaves
1 drained canned *jalapeño* pepper,
　　seeded, and cut into strips
1 onion, thinly sliced
1 cup white wine vinegar
1 cup olive or corn oil
salt

To garnish

lettuce leaves
green olives

1 Cut the fish fillets into eight pieces and arrange them in a single layer in a shallow dish. Drizzle with the lime juice. Cover and marinate for 15 minutes, turning the fillets once.

2 Lift out the fillets with a spatula, pat dry with paper towels and season with salt. Heat 4 tablespoons of the oil in a frying pan and sauté the fish until lightly golden brown. Transfer to a platter and set aside.

3 Combine the cloves, peppercorns, garlic, cumin, oregano, bay leaves, chili and vinegar in a pan. Bring to a boil, then simmer for 3–4 minutes.

4 Add the remaining oil, and bring to a simmer. Pour over the fish. Cool, cover and chill for 24 hours. To serve, lift out the fillets with a spatula and arrange on a serving dish. Garnish with lettuce and olives.

— COOK'S TIP —

To make the dish special, add an elaborate garnish of radishes, capers and chili strips.

Red Snapper, Veracruz-style

This is Mexico's best-known fish dish. In Veracruz, red snapper is always used but fillets of any firm-fleshed white fish can be substituted successfully.

INGREDIENTS

Serves 4

4 large red snapper fillets
2 tablespoons freshly squeezed lime or lemon juice
½ cup olive oil
1 onion, finely chopped
2 garlic cloves, chopped
1½ pounds tomatoes, peeled and chopped
1 bay leaf, plus a few sprigs for garnish
¼ teaspoon dried oregano
2 tablespoons large capers, plus extra to serve (optional)
16 pitted green olives, halved
2 drained canned *jalapeño* peppers, seeded and cut into strips
butter, for frying
3 slices firm white bread, cut into triangles
salt and freshly ground black pepper

1 Arrange the fish fillets in a single layer in a shallow dish. Season with salt and pepper, drizzle with the lime juice and set aside.

2 Heat the oil in a large frying pan and sauté the onion and garlic until the onion is soft. Add the tomatoes and cook for about 10 minutes until the mixture is thick and flavorful. Stir the mixture from time to time.

3 Stir in the bay leaf, oregano, capers, olives and chilies. Add the fish and cook over very low heat for about 10 minutes or until tender.

--- COOK'S TIP ---

This dish can also be made with a whole red snapper, weighing about 3–3½ pounds. Bake together with the sauce, in a pre-heated oven at 325°F. Allow 10 minutes cooking time for every 1 inch of the fish's thickness.

4 While the fish is cooking, heat the butter in a small frying pan and sauté the bread triangles until they are golden brown on both sides.

5 Transfer the fish to a heated platter, pour over the sauce and surround with the fried bread triangles. Garnish with bay leaves and serve with extra capers, if you like.

Shrimp with Chayote in Turmeric Sauce

Galangal, red chilies and turmeric add distinctive hot and spicy flavor to this tasty Indonesian dish.

INGREDIENTS

Serves 4

1–2 chayotes or 2–3 zucchini
2 fresh red chilies, seeded
1 onion, quartered
¼-inch piece fresh galangal, peeled
1 lemon grass stem, lower 2 inches sliced, top bruised
1 inch fresh turmeric, peeled
⅞ cup water
lemon juice
14-ounce can coconut milk
1 pound cooked, peeled shrimp
salt
red chili shreds, to garnish (optional)
boiled rice, to serve

1 Peel the chayotes, remove the seeds and cut into strips. If using zucchini, cut into 2-inch strips.

2 Grind the fresh red chilies, onion, sliced galangal, sliced lemon grass and the fresh turmeric to a paste in a food processor or with a pestle and mortar. Add the water to the paste mixture, with a squeeze of lemon juice and salt to taste.

3 Pour into a pan. Add the top of the lemon grass stem. Bring to the boil and cook for 1–2 minutes. Add the chayote or zucchini pieces and cook for 2 minutes. Stir in the coconut milk. Taste and adjust the seasoning.

4 Stir in the shrimp and cook gently for 2–3 minutes. Remove the lemon grass stem. Garnish with shreds of chili, if using, and serve with rice.

Indonesian Spicy Fish

Fish is given a hot, piquant twist in this flavorful dish.

INGREDIENTS

Serves 6–8

2¼ pounds fresh mackerel fillets, skinned
2 tablespoons tamarind pulp, soaked in ⅞ cup water
1 onion
½-inch piece fresh galangal
2 garlic cloves
1–2 fresh red chilies, seeded, or 1 teaspoon chili powder
1 teaspoon ground coriander
1 teaspoon ground turmeric
½ teaspoon ground fennel seeds
1 tablespoon dark brown sugar
6–7 tablespoons oil
⅞ cup coconut cream
salt and freshly ground black pepper
fresh chili shreds, to garnish

1 Rinse the fish fillets in cold water and dry them well on paper towels. Put into a shallow dish and sprinkle with a little salt. Strain the tamarind and pour the juice over the fish fillets. Set aside for 30 minutes.

2 Quarter the onion, peel and slice the galangal and peel the garlic. Grind the onion, galangal, garlic and chilies or chili powder to a paste in a food processor or with a pestle and mortar. Add the ground coriander, turmeric, fennel seeds and sugar.

3 Heat half of the oil in a frying pan. Drain the fish fillets and fry for 5 minutes, or until cooked. Set aside.

4 Wipe out the pan and heat the remaining oil. Fry the spice paste, stirring constantly, until it gives off a spicy aroma. Do not let it brown. Add the coconut cream and simmer gently for a few minutes. Add the fish fillets and gently heat through.

5 Taste for seasoning and serve sprinkled with shredded chili.

Braised Fish in Chili and Garlic Sauce

INGREDIENTS

Serves 4–6

1 bream or trout, 1½ pounds, gutted
1 tablespoon light soy sauce
1 tablespoon Chinese rice wine
vegetable oil, for deep-frying

For the sauce

2 garlic cloves, finely chopped
2–3 scallions, finely chopped
1 teaspoon chopped fresh ginger
2 tablespoons chili bean sauce
1 tablespoon tomato paste
2 teaspoons light brown sugar
1 tablespoon rice vinegar
about ½ cup fish stock
1 tablespoon cornstarch paste
few drops sesame oil

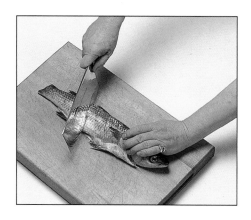

1 Rinse and dry the fish well. Using a sharp knife, score both sides of the fish as far down as the bone with diagonal cuts about 1 inch apart. Rub the whole fish with soy sauce and wine on both sides, then marinate it for 10–15 minutes.

2 In a wok, deep-fry the fish in hot oil for about 3–4 minutes on both sides until golden brown.

3 Pour off the excess oil, leaving a thin layer in the wok. Push the fish to one side of the wok and add the garlic, the white part of the scallions, fresh ginger, chili bean sauce, tomato paste, brown sugar, rice vinegar and stock. Bring to a boil and braise the fish in the sauce for about 4–5 minutes, turning it over once. Add the green part of the chopped scallions. Thicken the sauce with the cornstarch paste, sprinkle with the sesame oil and place on a dish to serve immediately.

--- VARIATION ---

Any whole fish is suitable for this dish; try sea bass, grouper or gray mullet, if you like. Also, if you can't find Chinese wine, use dry sherry instead.

Salt Cod in Mild Chili Sauce

INGREDIENTS

Serves 6

2 pounds dried salt cod
1 onion, chopped
2 garlic cloves, chopped
1 fresh green chili, sliced, to garnish

For the sauce

6 dried *ancho* chilies
1 onion, chopped
½ teaspoon dried oregano
½ teaspoon ground coriander
1 *serrano* chili, seeded and chopped
3 tablespoons corn oil
3 cups fish or chicken stock
salt

--- Cook's Tip ---

Dried salt cod is a great favorite in Spain and Portugal and throughout Latin America. Look for it in Spanish and Portuguese markets.

1 Soak the cod in cold water for several hours, depending on how hard and salty it is. Change the water once or twice during soaking.

2 Drain the fish and transfer it to a saucepan. Pour in water to cover. Bring to a gentle simmer and cook for about 15 minutes, until the fish is tender. Drain, reserving the stock. Remove any skin or bones from the fish and cut it into 1½-inch pieces.

3 Make the sauce. Remove the stems and shake out the seeds from the *ancho* chilies. Tear the pods into pieces, put in a bowl of warm water and soak until they are soft.

4 Drain the soaked chilies and put them into a food processor with the onion, oregano, coriander and *serrano* chili. Process to a purée.

5 Heat the oil in a frying pan and cook the purée, stirring, for about 5 minutes. Stir in the fish or chicken stock and simmer for 3–4 minutes.

6 Add the prepared cod and simmer for a few minutes longer to heat the fish through and blend the flavors. Serve garnished with the sliced chili.

Baked or Grilled Spiced Whole Fish

INGREDIENTS

Serves 6

2¼ pounds red snapper or striped bass,
   cleaned and scaled if necessary
1 fresh red chili, seeded and ground, or
   1 teaspoon minced chili from a jar
4 garlic cloves, crushed
1 inch fresh ginger root, sliced
4 scallions, chopped
juice of ½ lemon
2 tablespoons sunflower oil
salt
boiled rice, to serve

1 Rinse the fish and dry it well inside and out with paper towels. Using a sharp knife, slash two or three times through the fleshy part on each side of the fish.

2 Place the chili, garlic, ginger and spring onions in a food processor and blend to a paste, or grind the mixture together with a mortar and pestle. Add the lemon juice and salt, then stir in the oil.

3 Spoon a little of the mixture inside the fish and pour the rest over the top. Turn the fish to coat it completely in the spice mixture and leave to marinate for at least an hour.

4 Preheat the broiler. Place a long strip of double foil under the fish to support it and to make turning it over easier. Put on a rack in the broiler and cook for 5 minutes on one side and 8 minutes on the second side, basting with the marinade during cooking. Serve with boiled rice.

Vinegar Chili Fish

INGREDIENTS

Serves 2–3

2–3 medium-size mackerel, filleted
2–3 fresh red chilies, seeded
4 macadamia nuts or 8 almonds
1 red onion, quartered
2 garlic cloves, crushed
½ inch fresh ginger root, peeled
   and sliced
1 teaspoon ground turmeric
3 tablespoons coconut or vegetable oil
3 tablespoons wine vinegar
⅝ cup water
salt
Deep-fried Onions, to garnish
finely chopped fresh chili, to garnish

1 Rinse the fish fillets in cold water and then dry them well on paper towels. Set aside.

2 Grind the chilies, nuts, onion, garlic, ginger, turmeric and 1 tablespoon of the oil to a paste in a food processor or with a mortar and pestle. Heat the remaining oil in a frying pan and cook the paste for 1–2 minutes without browning. Stir in the vinegar and water. Add salt to taste. Bring to a boil, then simmer.

3 Place the fish fillets in the sauce. Cover and cook for 6–8 minutes, or until the fish is tender.

4 Lift the fish onto a plate and keep warm. Reduce the sauce by boiling rapidly for 1 minute. Pour over the fish and serve. Garnish with Deep-fried Onions and chopped chili.

Mexican Spicy Fish

This is a typical Mexican dish.

Ingredients

Serves 6

3 – 3½ pounds striped bass or any non-oily white fish, cut into 6 steaks
½ cup corn oil
1 large onion, thinly sliced
2 garlic cloves, chopped
12 ounces tomatoes, sliced
2 drained canned *jalapeño* peppers, rinsed and sliced
flat-leaf parsley, to garnish

For the marinade

4 garlic cloves, crushed
1 teaspoon black peppercorns
1 teaspoon dried oregano
½ teaspoon ground cumin
1 teaspoon ground *achiote* (annatto)
½ teaspoon ground cinnamon
½ cup mild white vinegar
salt

1 Arrange the fish steaks in a single layer in a shallow dish. Make the marinade. Using a pestle, grind the garlic and black peppercorns in a mortar. Add the dried oregano, cumin, *achiote* (annatto) and cinnamon and mix to a paste with the vinegar. Add salt to taste and spread the marinade on both sides of each of the fish steaks. Cover and let sit in a cool place for 1 hour.

2 Select a flameproof dish large enough to hold the fish in a single layer, and pour in enough of the oil to coat the bottom. Arrange the fish in the dish with any remaining marinade.

3 Top the fish with the onion, garlic, tomatoes and chilies and pour the rest of the oil over the top.

4 Cover the dish and cook over low heat on top of the stove for 15 – 20 minutes, or until the fish is no longer translucent. Serve at once garnished with flat leaf parsley.

Citrus Fish with Chilies

INGREDIENTS

Serves 4

4 halibut or cod steaks or fillets, about
   6 ounces each
juice of 1 lemon
1 teaspoon garlic powder
1 teaspoon paprika
1 teaspoon ground cumin
¾ teaspoon dried tarragon
4 tablespoons olive oil
flour, for dusting
1¼ cups fish stock
2 red chilies, seeded and finely chopped
2 tablespoons chopped fresh cilantro
1 red onion, cut into rings
salt and freshly ground black pepper

1 Place the fish in a shallow bowl and mix together the lemon juice, garlic, paprika, cumin, tarragon and a little salt and pepper. Spoon over the lemon mixture, cover loosely with plastic wrap and allow to marinate for a few hours or overnight in the fridge.

2 Gently heat all of the oil in a large nonstick frying pan, dust the fish with flour and then fry the fish for a few minutes on each side, until golden brown all over.

3 Pour the fish stock around the fish, and simmer, covered, for about 5 minutes or until the fish is thoroughly cooked through.

4 Add the chopped red chilies and 1 tablespoon of the cilantro to the pan. Simmer for 5 minutes.

5 Transfer the fish and sauce to a serving plate and keep warm.

6 Wipe out the pan, add and heat some olive oil and stir fry the onion rings until speckled brown. Sprinkle over the fish with the remaining chopped cilantro and serve at once.

Saffron Fish

INGREDIENTS

Serves 4
2–3 saffron strands
2 egg yolks
1 garlic clove, crushed
4 salmon trout steaks
oil for deep frying
salt and ground black pepper
green salad, to serve

1 Soak the saffron in 1 tablespoon boiling water and then beat the mixture into the egg yolks. Season with garlic, salt and pepper.

COOK'S TIP

Any type of fish can be used in this recipe. Try a combination of plain and smoked for a delicious change, such as salmon or smoked and unsmoked cod.

2 Place the fish steaks in a shallow dish and coat with the egg mixture. Cover with plastic wrap and marinate for up to 1 hour.

3 Heat the oil in a deep fryer until it's very hot and then fry the fish, one steak at a time, for about 10 minutes until golden brown. Drain each one on paper towels. Serve with Rice with Fresh Herbs, lemon wedges and a green salad.

Pan-fried Spicy Sardines

This delicious fish recipe is a favorite in many Arab countries.

INGREDIENTS

Serves 4
1 tablespoon fresh parsley
3–4 garlic cloves, crushed
8–12 sardines, prepared
2 tablespoons lemon juice
½ cup flour
1 teaspoon ground cumin
4 tablespoons vegetable oil
salt and freshly ground black pepper
nan bread and salad, to serve

COOK'S TIP

Fresh sardines can be found in Portuguese markets and frozen fish are quite common in good supermarkets.

1 Finely chop the parsley and mix in a small bowl with the garlic.

2 Pat the parsley and garlic mixture all over the outsides and insides of the sardines. Sprinkle them with the lemon juice and set aside, covered, in a cool place for about 2 hours to absorb the flavors.

3 Place the flour on a large plate and season with cumin, salt and pepper. Roll the sardines in the flour, taking care to coat each fish thoroughly.

4 Heat the oil in a large frying pan and fry the fish in batches for 5 minutes on each side until crisp. Keep warm in the oven while cooking the remaining fish and then serve with nan bread and salad.

Whole Fish with Sweet and Sour Sauce

INGREDIENTS

Serves 4

1 whole fish, such as red snapper or
    carp, about 2¼ pounds prepared
2–3 tablespoons cornstarch
oil for frying
salt and freshly ground black pepper
boiled rice, to serve

For the spice paste

2 garlic cloves
2 lemon grass stems
1-inch piece fresh galangal, peeled
1 inch fresh ginger root
¾ inch fresh turmeric or
    ½ teaspoon ground turmeric
5 macadamia nuts or 10 almonds

For the sauce

1 tablespoon brown sugar
3 tablespoons cider vinegar
about 1½ cups water
2 lime leaves, torn
4 shallots, quartered
3 tomatoes, skinned and cut in wedges
3 scallions, finely shredded
1 fresh red chili, seeded and shredded

1 Wash and dry the fish thoroughly and then sprinkle it inside and out with salt. Set aside for 15 minutes, while preparing the other ingredients.

2 Peel and crush the garlic cloves. Use only the lower white part of the lemon grass stems and slice thinly. Peel and slice the fresh galangal, the fresh ginger and fresh turmeric and grind to a fine paste in a food processor or with a pestle and mortar.

3 Scrape the paste into a bowl. Stir in the brown sugar, cider vinegar, seasoning to taste and the water. Add the lime leaves.

4 Dust the fish with the cornstarch and fry on both sides in hot oil for about 8–9 minutes or until almost cooked through. Drain the fish on paper towels and transfer to a serving dish. Keep warm.

5 Pour off most of the oil and then pour in the spicy liquid and allow to come to a boil. Reduce the heat and cook for 3–4 minutes. Add the shallots and tomatoes, followed a minute later by the scallions and chili. Taste and adjust the seasoning.

6 Pour the sauce over the fish. Serve at once, with plenty of rice.

Turkish Cold Fish

Green chili, garlic and paprika add subtle spicing to this delicious fish dish. Cold fish is enjoyed in many parts of the Middle East – this particular version is from Turkey.

INGREDIENTS

Serves 4

4 tablespoons olive oil
2 pounds porgy or snapper
2 onions, sliced
1 green chili, seeded and chopped
1 red bell pepper, seeded and sliced
3 garlic cloves, crushed
1 tablespoon tomato paste
¼ cup fish stock, bottled clam juice
 or water
5–6 tomatoes, peeled and sliced or
 14-ounce can tomatoes
2 tablespoons chopped fresh parsley
2 tablespoons lemon juice
1 teaspoon paprika
15–20 green and black olives
salt and freshly ground black pepper
bread and salad, to serve

1 Heat 2 tablespoons of the oil in a large roasting pan or frying pan and fry the fish on both sides until golden brown. Remove from the tin or pan, cover and keep warm.

COOK'S TIP

One large fish looks spectacular, but it is tricky to both cook and serve. If you prefer, buy four smaller fish and cook for a shorter time, until just tender and cooked through but not overdone.

2 Heat the remaining oil in the tin or pan and fry the onions for 2–3 minutes until slightly softened. Add the chili and bell pepper and continue cooking for 3–4 minutes, stirring occasionally, then add the garlic and stir-fry for a further minute.

3 Blend the tomato paste with the fish stock, clam juice or water and stir into the pan with the tomatoes, parsley, lemon juice, paprika and seasoning. Simmer very gently for 15 minutes, stirring occasionally.

4 Return the fish to the pan and cover with the sauce. Cook for 10 minutes, then add the olives and cook for another 5 minutes or until just cooked through.

5 Transfer the fish to a serving dish and pour the sauce over the top. Allow to cool, then cover and chill until completely cold. Serve cold with bread and salad.

Jumbo Shrimp in Curry Sauce

INGREDIENTS

Serves 4
1 pound raw jumbo shrimp
2½ cups water
3 thin slices fresh ginger
2 teaspoons curry powder
2 garlic cloves, crushed
1 tablespoon butter or margarine
4 tablespoons ground almonds
1 green chili, seeded and finely
   chopped
3 tablespoons light cream
salt and freshly ground black pepper

For the vegetables

1 tablespoon mustard oil
1 tablespoon vegetable oil
1 onion, sliced
½ red bell pepper, seeded and thinly
   sliced
½ green bell pepper, seeded and thinly
   sliced
1 chayote, peeled, pitted and cut into
   strips
salt and freshly ground black pepper

1 Shell the shrimp and place the shells in a saucepan with the water and ginger. Simmer, uncovered, for 15 minutes until reduced by half. Strain into a pitcher and discard the shells.

2 Devein the shrimp, place in a bowl and season with the curry powder, garlic and salt and pepper and set aside.

3 Heat the mustard and vegetable oils in a large frying pan, add all the vegetables and stir fry for 5 minutes. Season with salt and pepper, spoon into a serving dish and keep warm.

4 Wipe out the frying pan, then add and melt the butter or margarine and sauté the shrimp for about 5 minutes or until pink. Spoon over the bed of vegetables, cover and keep warm.

5 Add the ground almonds and chili to the pan, stir fry for a few seconds and then add the reserved stock and bring to a boil. Reduce the heat, stir in the cream and simmer for a few minutes, without boiling.

6 Pour the sauce over the vegetables and shrimp before serving.

Fried Fish in Green Chili Sauce

INGREDIENTS

Serves 4
4 medium porgy or butterfish
juice of 1 lemon
1 teaspoon garlic powder
salt and freshly ground black pepper
vegetable oil, for shallow frying

For the coconut sauce

1⅞ cups water
2 thin slices fresh ginger
1 cup coconut cream
2 tablespoons vegetable oil
1 red onion, sliced
2 garlic cloves, crushed
1 green chili, seeded and thinly sliced
1 tablespoon chopped fresh cilantro
salt and freshly ground black pepper

1 Cut the fish in half and sprinkle inside and out with the lemon juice. Season with the garlic powder and salt and pepper and set aside to marinate for a few hours.

2 Heat a little oil in a large frying pan. Pat off the excess lemon juice from the fish, fry in the oil for 10 minutes, turning once. Set aside.

3 To make the sauce, place the water in a saucepan with the slices of ginger, bring to a boil and simmer until the liquid is reduced to just over 1¼ cups. Take out the ginger and reserve, then add the coconut cream to the pan and stir until the coconut has been absorbed.

4 Heat the oil in a wok or large pan and fry the onion and garlic for 2–3 minutes. Add the reserved ginger and coconut stock, the chili and cilantro, stir well and then gently lower in the fish. Simmer for 10 minutes, until the fish is cooked through. Transfer the fish to a warmed serving plate, adjust the seasoning for the sauce and pour over the fish. Serve immediately.

Chili Crabs

There are variations on this recipe all over Asia, but all are hot and spicy. This delicious dish owes its spiciness and flavor to chilies, ginger and shrimp paste.

INGREDIENTS

Serves 4

2 cooked crabs, about 1½ pounds
½-inch cube shrimp paste
2 garlic cloves
2 fresh red chilies, seeded, or
   1 teaspoon chopped chili from a jar
½ inch fresh ginger root, peeled
   and sliced
4 tablespoons sunflower oil
1¼ cups tomato ketchup
1 tablespoon dark brown sugar
½ cup warm water
4 scallions, chopped, to garnish
cucumber chunks and hot toast,
   to serve (optional)

1 Remove the large claws of one crab and turn onto its back with the head facing away from you. Use your thumbs to push the body up from the main shell. Discard the stomach sac and "dead men's fingers," i.e. lungs and any green matter. Leave the creamy brown meat in the shell and cut the shell in half with a cleaver or heavy knife. Cut the body section in half and crack the claws with a sharp blow from a hammer or cleaver. Avoid splintering the claws. Repeat with the other crab.

2 Grind the shrimp paste, garlic, chilies and ginger to a paste with a pestle and mortar.

3 Heat a wok and add the oil. Fry the spice paste, stirring it constantly, without browning.

4 Stir in the tomato ketchup, sugar and water and mix the sauce well. When just boiling, add all the crab pieces and toss in the sauce until well-coated and hot. Serve in a large bowl, sprinkled with the spring onions. Place in the center of the table for everyone to help themselves. Accompany this finger-licking dish with cool cucumber chunks and hot toast for mopping up the sauce, if you like.

Caribbean Spiced Fish

This dish is of Spanish origin and is very popular throughout the Caribbean. There are as many variations of the name of the dish as there are ways of preparing it.

INGREDIENTS

Serves 4–6
2 pounds red snapper fillet
½ lemon
1 tablespoon spice seasoning
flour, for dusting
oil, for frying
lemon wedges, to garnish

For the sauce

2 tablespoons vegetable oil
1 onion, sliced
½ red bell pepper, sliced
½ chayote, peeled and seeded, cut into
   small pieces
2 garlic cloves, crushed
½ cup malt vinegar
5 tablespoons water
½ teaspoon ground allspice
1 bay leaf
1 small Scotch Bonnet pepper, chopped
1 tablespoon brown sugar
salt and freshly ground black pepper

1 Place the fish in a shallow dish, squeeze over the lemon, then sprinkle with the spice seasoning and pat into the fish. Let marinate in a cool place for at least 1 hour.

2 Cut the fish into 3-inch pieces and dust with a little flour, shaking off the excess.

3 Heat the oil in a heavy frying pan and fry the fish pieces for 2–3 minutes until golden brown and crisp, turning occasionally. To make the sauce, heat the oil in a heavy frying pan and fry the onion until soft.

4 Add the pepper, chayote and garlic and stir-fry for 2 minutes. Pour in the vinegar, then add the remaining ingredients and simmer gently for 5 minutes. Let stand for 10 minutes, then pour over the fish. Serve hot, garnished with lemon wedges.

—————— COOK'S TIP ——————

In the Caribbean, whole fish are used for this dish but fillets are also fine.

Shrimp in Spicy Tomato Sauce

Cumin and cinnamon add subtle spiciness to this delicious, simple-to-make shrimp recipe, which comes from the Middle East.

INGREDIENTS

Serves 4
2 tablespoons oil
2 onions, finely chopped
2–3 garlic cloves, crushed
5–6 tomatoes, peeled and chopped
2 tablespoons tomato paste
½ cup fish stock
  or water
½ teaspoon ground cumin
½ teaspoon ground cinnamon
1 pound raw, peeled medium to
  large shrimp
juice of 1 lemon
salt and freshly ground black pepper
fresh parsley, to garnish
rice, to serve

1 Heat the oil in a large frying pan or saucepan and fry the onions for 3–4 minutes until golden. Add the garlic, fry for about 1 minute, and then stir in the tomatoes.

2 Blend the tomato paste with the stock or water and stir into the pan with the cumin, cinnamon and seasoning. Simmer, covered, over a low heat for 15 minutes, stirring occasionally. Do not allow to boil.

3 Add the shrimp and lemon juice and simmer the sauce for another 10–15 minutes over a low to moderate heat until the shrimp are cooked and the stock is reduced by about half.

4 Serve with plain rice or in a decorative ring of Persian rice, garnished with parsley.

Spiced Fish Kebabs

Marinating adds spicy flavor to these delicious kebabs.

INGREDIENTS

Serves 4–6
2 pounds swordfish steaks
3 tablespoons olive oil
juice of ½ lemon
1 garlic clove, crushed
1 teaspoon cayenne pepper
3 tomatoes, quartered
2 onions, cut into wedges
salt and freshly ground black pepper
salad and pita bread, to serve

--- COOK'S TIP ---

Almost any type of firm white fish can be used for this recipe.

1 Cut the fish into large cubes and place in a dish.

2 Blend together the oil, lemon juice, garlic, cayenne pepper and seasoning in a small mixing bowl. Pour over the fish. Cover loosely with plastic wrap and let marinate in a cool place for up to 2 hours.

3 Thread the fish cubes onto skewers, alternating with pieces of tomato and onion.

4 Grill the kebabs over hot charcoal for 5–10 minutes, basting frequently with the remaining marinade and turning occasionally. Serve with salad and pita bread.

Shrimp in Spiced Coconut Sauce

Spices, chilies and herbs make a fragrant sauce for this dish.

INGREDIENTS

Serves 4

24–30 large raw shrimp, shelled
spice seasoning, for dusting
juice of 1 lemon
2 tablespoons butter or margarine
1 onion, chopped
2 garlic cloves, crushed
2 tablespoons tomato paste
½ teaspoon dried thyme
½ teaspoon ground cinnamon
1 tablespoon chopped fresh cilantro
½ hot chili pepper, chopped
6 ounces frozen or canned corn
1¼ cups coconut milk
chopped fresh cilantro, to garnish

1 Sprinkle the shrimp with spice seasoning and lemon juice and marinate in a cool place for an hour.

2 Melt the butter or margarine in a saucepan, fry the onion and garlic for 5 minutes, until slightly softened. Add the shrimp and cook for a few minutes, stirring occasionally until cooked through and pink.

3 Transfer the shrimp, onion and garlic to a bowl, leaving behind some of the buttery liquid. Add the tomato paste and cook over a low heat, stirring well. Add the thyme, cinnamon, cilantro and hot pepper and stir well.

4 Blend the corn (reserving about 1 tablespoon) in a blender or food processor with the coconut milk. Add to the pan and simmer until reduced. Add the shrimp and reserved corn, and simmer for 5 minutes. Serve hot, garnished with cilantro.

--- COOK'S TIP ---

If you use raw jumbo shrimp, make a stock from the shells and use in place of some of the coconut milk.

Curried Shrimp and Saltfish

Shrimp paste and spices add tasty flavor to this fish dish.

INGREDIENTS

Serves 4

1 pound raw shrimp, peeled and
  deveined
1 tablespoon spice seasoning
2 tablespoons butter or margarine
1 tablespoon olive oil
2 shallots, finely chopped
1 garlic clove, crushed
12 ounces okra, and cut into 1-inch
  lengths
1 teaspoon curry powder
1 teaspoon shrimp paste
2 tablespoons chopped fresh cilantro
1 tablespoon lemon juice
6 ounces prepared salt cod (see Cook's
  Tip), shredded

1 Season the shrimp with the spice seasoning and let marinate in a cool place for about 1 hour.

2 Heat the butter or margarine and olive oil in a large frying pan or wok over a moderate heat and stir-fry the shallots and garlic for 5 minutes. Add the okra, curry powder and shrimp paste, stir well and cook for about 10 minutes, until the okra is tender.

3 Add 2 tablespoons water, cilantro, lemon juice, shrimp and salt cod, and cook gently for 5–10 minutes. Adjust the seasoning and serve hot.

--- COOK'S TIP ---

Soak the salt fish for 12 hours, changing the water two or three times. Rinse, bring to a boil in fresh water, then cool.

Lemon Grass Shrimp on Crisp Noodle Cake

INGREDIENTS

Serves 4

11 ounces thin egg noodles
4 tablespoons vegetable oil
1¼ pounds raw jumbo shrimp, peeled
   and deveined
½ teaspoon ground coriander
1 tablespoon ground turmeric
2 garlic cloves, finely chopped
2 slices fresh ginger, finely chopped
2 lemon grass stalks, finely chopped
2 shallots, finely chopped
1 tablespoon tomato paste
1 cup coconut cream
4–6 kaffir lime leaves (optional)
1–2 tablespoons fresh lime juice
1–2 tablespoons fish sauce
1 cucumber, peeled, seeded and cut
   into 2-inch batons
1 tomato, seeded and cut into strips
2 red chilies, seeded and finely sliced
salt and freshly ground black pepper
2 scallions, finely sliced, and a few
   cilantro sprigs, to garnish

1 Cook the egg noodles in a saucepan of boiling water until just tender. Drain, rinse under cold running water, and drain well.

2 Heat 1 tablespoon of the oil in a large frying pan. Add the noodles, distributing them evenly, and fry for 4–5 minutes until crisp and golden. Turn the noodle cake over, and fry the other side. Alternatively, make four individual cakes. Keep hot.

3 In a bowl, toss the shrimp with the ground coriander, turmeric, garlic, ginger and lemon grass. Add salt and pepper to taste.

4 Heat the remaining oil in a large frying pan. Add the shallots, fry for 1 minute, then add the shrimp, and fry for 2 minutes more. Using a slotted spoon, remove the shrimp.

5 Stir the tomato paste and coconut cream into the mixture remaining in the pan. Stir in lime juice to taste, and season with the fish sauce. Bring the sauce to a simmer, return the shrimp to the sauce, then add the kaffir lime leaves, if using, and the cucumber. Simmer gently until the shrimp is cooked, and the sauce is reduced to a nice coating consistency.

6 Add the tomato, stir until just warmed through, then add the chilies. Serve on top of the crisp noodle cake(s), garnished with sliced scallions and cilantro sprigs.

Stir-fried Shrimp with Tamarind

The sour, tangy flavor that is characteristic of many Thai dishes comes from tamarind. Fresh tamarind pods, from the tamarind tree, can sometimes be bought, but preparing them for cooking is a laborious process. The Thais prefer to use compressed blocks of tamarind paste, which is simply soaked in warm water and then strained.

INGREDIENTS

Serves 4–6
2 tablespoons tamarind paste
⅔ cup boiling water
2 tablespoons vegetable oil
2 tablespoons chopped onion
2 tablespoons palm sugar
2 tablespoons chicken stock or water
1 tablespoon fish sauce
6 dried red chilies, fried
1 pound uncooked shelled shrimp
1 tablespoon fried chopped garlic
2 tablespoons fried sliced shallots
2 scallions, chopped, to garnish

1 Put the tamarind paste in a small bowl, pour over the boiling water and stir well to break up any lumps. Set aside for 30 minutes. Strain, pushing as much of the juice through as possible. Measure 6 tablespoons of the juice, which is the amount needed, and store the rest in the fridge. Heat the oil in a wok. Add the chopped onion and fry until golden brown.

2 Add the sugar, stock, fish sauce, dried chilies and the tamarind juice, stirring well until the sugar dissolves. Bring to a boil.

3 Add the shrimp, garlic and shallots. Stir-fry for about 3–4 minutes until the shrimp are cooked. Garnish with the chopped scallions.

Spicy Shrimp with Okra

INGREDIENTS

Serves 4–6

4–6 tablespoons oil
8 ounces okra, washed, dried and
  left whole
4 garlic cloves, crushed
2-inch piece of fresh ginger, chopped
4–6 green chilies, cut diagonally
½ teaspoon turmeric
4–6 curry leaves
1 teaspoon cumin seeds
1 pound fresh jumbo shrimp, shelled
  and deveined
2 teaspoons brown sugar
juice of 2 lemons
salt, to taste

1 Heat the oil in a frying pan and fry the okra on fairly high heat until they are slightly crisp and browned on all sides. Remove from the oil and keep aside on paper towels.

2 In the same oil, gently fry the garlic, ginger, chilies, turmeric, curry leaves and cumin seeds for 2–3 minutes. Add the shrimp and mix well. Cook until the shrimp are tender.

3 Add the salt, sugar, lemon juice and fried okra. Increase the heat and quickly fry for 5 minutes more, stirring gently to prevent the okra from breaking. Adjust the seasoning, if necessary. Serve hot.

COOK'S TIP

Okra should be cooked rapidly to prevent the pods from breaking up and releasing their distinctive thick, sticky liquid.

Spicy Shrimp with Cornmeal

These crispy fried shrimp with a cornmeal coating and a cheesy topping are truly delicious when served with a spicy tomato salsa.

INGREDIENTS

Serves 4

3/4 cup cornmeal
1–2 teaspoons cayenne pepper
1/2 teaspoon ground cumin
1 teaspoon salt
2 tablespoons chopped fresh cilantro or parsley
2 pounds large raw Gulf shrimp, shelled and deveined
flour, for dredging
1/4 cup vegetable oil
1 cup shredded Monterey Jack or Cheddar cheese

To serve
lime wedges
tomato salsa

1 Preheat the broiler. In a mixing bowl, combine the cornmeal, cayenne pepper, cumin, salt and cilantro or parsley.

2 Coat the shrimp lightly in flour, then dip them in water and roll them in the cornmeal mixture to coat.

3 Heat the oil in a nonstick frying pan. When hot, add the shrimp, in batches if necessary. Cook them until they are opaque throughout, for about 2–3 minutes on each side. Drain on paper towels.

4 Place the shrimp in a large baking dish, or in individual dishes. Sprinkle the cheese evenly over the top. Broil about 3 inches from the heat until the cheese melts, for about 2–3 minutes. Serve immediately, with lime wedges and tomato salsa.

Pineapple Curry with Shrimp and Mussels

The delicate sweet-and-sour flavor of this curry comes from the pineapple and, although it seems an odd combination, it is rather delicious. Use the freshest shellfish that you can find.

INGREDIENTS

Serves 4–6

2½ cups unsweetened coconut milk
2 tablespoons red curry paste
2 tablespoons fish sauce
1 tablespoon sugar
8 ounces jumbo shrimp, shelled and deveined
1 pound mussels, cleaned and beards removed
6 ounces fresh pineapple, finely crushed or chopped
5 kaffir lime leaves, torn
2 red chilies, chopped, and cilantro leaves, to garnish

1 In a large saucepan, bring half the coconut milk to a boil and heat, stirring, until it separates.

2 Add the red curry paste and cook until fragrant. Add the fish sauce and sugar and continue to cook for a few moments.

3 Stir in the rest of the coconut milk and bring back to a boil. Add the jumbo shrimp, mussels, pineapple and kaffir lime leaves.

4 Reheat until boiling and then simmer for 3–5 minutes, until the shrimp are cooked and the mussels have opened. Remove any mussels that have not opened and discard. Serve garnished with chopped red chilies and cilantro leaves.

Curried Shrimp in Coconut Milk

A curry-like dish where the shrimp are cooked in a spicy coconut gravy.

INGREDIENTS

Serves 4–6

2½ cups unsweetened coconut milk
2 tablespoons yellow curry paste (see Cook's Tip)
1 tablespoon fish sauce
½ teaspoon salt
1 teaspoon sugar
1 pound jumbo shrimp, shelled, tails left intact and deveined
8 ounces cherry tomatoes
juice of ½ lime, to serve
2 red chilies, cut into strips, and cilantro leaves, to garnish

1 Put half the coconut milk into a pan or wok and bring to a boil.

2 Add the yellow curry paste to the coconut milk, stir until it disperses, then simmer for about 10 minutes.

3 Add the fish sauce, salt, sugar and remaining coconut milk. Simmer for another 5 minutes.

4 Add the shrimp and cherry tomatoes. Simmer very gently for about 5 minutes until the shrimp are pink and tender.

5 Serve sprinkled with lime juice and garnished with chilies and cilantro.

> — COOK'S TIP —
>
> To make yellow curry paste, process 6–8 yellow chilies, 1 chopped lemongrass stalk, 4 peeled shallots, 4 garlic cloves, 1 tablespoon peeled chopped fresh ginger, 1 teaspoon coriander seeds, 1 teaspoon mustard powder, 1 teaspoon salt, ½ teaspoon ground cinnamon, 1 tablespoon light brown sugar and 2 tablespoons oil in a blender or food processor. When a paste forms, transfer to a jar and keep in the fridge.

SCORCHING MEAT AND POULTRY

Meat and poultry dishes cooked with chilies and spices are universally popular, but recipe variations are endless and each country adds its own twist and unique mixture of spices; Blackened Hot Chicken Breasts from the deep South, Caribbean Barbecued Jerk Chicken, Beef Enchiladas from Mexico and Spicy Meat Fritters from Indonesia are just a few of the fiery dishes on offer.

Spicy Meat Fritters

INGREDIENTS

Makes 30

1 pound potatoes, boiled and drained
1 pound lean ground beef
1 onion, quartered
1 bunch scallions, chopped
3 garlic cloves, crushed
1 teaspoon ground nutmeg
1 tablespoon coriander seeds, dry-fried
   and ground
2 teaspoons cumin seeds, dry-fried
   and ground
4 eggs, beaten
oil for shallow-frying
salt and freshly ground black pepper

1 While the potatoes are still warm, mash them in the pan until they are well broken up. Add to the ground beef and mix well together.

2 Finely chop the onion, scallions and garlic. Add to the meat with the ground nutmeg, coriander and cumin. Stir in enough beaten egg to give a soft consistency which can be formed into fritters. Season to taste.

3 Heat the oil in a large frying pan. Using a dessertspoon, scoop out 6–8 oval-shaped fritters and drop them into the hot oil. Allow to set, so that they keep their shape (this will take about 3 minutes) and then turn over and cook for another minute.

4 Drain well on paper towels and keep warm while cooking the remaining fritters.

Barbecued Pork Spareribs

INGREDIENTS

Serves 4

2¼ pounds pork spareribs
1 onion
2 garlic cloves
1 inch fresh ginger root
⅓ cup dark soy sauce
1–2 fresh red chilies, seeded
   and chopped
1 teaspoon tamarind pulp, soaked in
   ⅓ cup water
1–2 tablespoons dark brown sugar
2 tablespoons peanut oil
salt and freshly ground black pepper

1 Wipe the pork ribs and place them in a wok, wide frying pan or large flameproof casserole.

2 Finely chop the onion, crush the garlic and peel and slice the ginger. Blend the soy sauce, onion, garlic, ginger and chopped chilies together to a paste in a food processor or with a mortar and pestle. Strain the tamarind and reserve the juice. Add the tamarind juice, brown sugar, oil and seasoning to taste to the onion mixture and mix well together.

3 Pour the sauce over the ribs and toss well to coat. Bring to a boil and then simmer, uncovered and stirring frequently, for 30 minutes. Add extra water if necessary.

4 Put the ribs on a rack in a roasting pan, place under a preheated broiler, on a barbecue grill or in the oven at 400°F. Continue cooking until the ribs are tender, about 20 minutes, depending on the thickness of the ribs. Baste the ribs with the sauce and turn them over from time to time.

Beef with Cactus Pieces

Nopalitos – edible cactus chunks – are used widely in Mexico, and are the basis of several salads, soups and casseroles.

Ingredients

Serves 6

2 pounds braising beef, cut into 2-inch cubes
2 tablespoons corn oil
1 onion, finely chopped
2 garlic cloves, chopped
1 or 2 *jalapeño* peppers, seeded and chopped
1 can (4 ounces) *nopalitos* (cactus pieces), rinsed and drained
2 cans (10 ounces each) tomatillos (Mexican green tomatoes)
1/2 cup chopped fresh cilantro
beef stock (optional)
salt and freshly ground black pepper
chopped fresh cilantro, to garnish

1 Pat the beef cubes dry with paper towels. Heat the oil in a frying pan and sauté the beef cubes a few at a time, until browned all over. Using a slotted spoon, transfer the beef cubes to a flameproof casserole or pan.

2 Add the onion and garlic to the oil remaining in the frying pan and sauté until the onion is tender. Add more oil, if necessary. Add the onions and garlic to the casserole, along with the *jalapeños.*

3 Add the *nopalitos* and tomatillos, with the can juices, to the casserole. Stir in the cilantro until well mixed. If more liquid is needed to cover the beef, stir in as much stock as needed. Season with salt and pepper.

4 Bring to a slow simmer, cover and cook over low heat for about 2¹/₂ hours, or until the beef is very tender. Serve sprinkled with the chopped cilantro.

Cook's Tip

Tomatillos (Mexican green tomatoes) are not to be confused with ordinary green, unripe, tomatoes. Look for them canned, in most supermarkets. Fresh tomatillos are also widely available.

Tex-Mex Baked Potatoes with Chili

INGREDIENTS

Serves 4

2 large potatoes
1 tablespoon oil
1 garlic clove, minced
1 small onion, chopped
½ red bell pepper, seeded and chopped
8 ounces lean ground beef
½ fresh red chili, seeded and chopped
1 teaspoon ground cumin
pinch of cayenne pepper
7-ounce can chopped tomatoes
2 tablespoons tomato paste
½ teaspoon dried oregano
½ teaspoon dried marjoram
7-ounce can red kidney beans
1 tablespoon chopped fresh cilantro
4 tablespoons sour cream
salt and ground black pepper
chopped fresh parsley, to garnish

1 Preheat the oven to 425°F. Rub oil all over the potatoes and pierce with skewers. Bake for 30 minutes.

2 Heat the oil in a pan and add the garlic, onion and pepper. Fry gently for 4–5 minutes until softened.

3 Add the ground beef, and fry until it is browned all over, then stir in the chopped chili, ground cumin, cayenne pepper, tomatoes, tomato paste, 4 tablespoons water and the herbs. Cover and simmer for about 25 minutes, stirring occasionally.

VARIATION

For a lower fat topping, use plain yogurt instead of sour cream.

4 Drain the kidney beans and add to the pan. Cook for 5 minutes, turn off the heat and stir in the chopped cilantro. Season well and set aside.

5 Cut the baked potatoes in half and place one half in each of four serving bowls. Top them with the chili beef mixture and a dollop of sour cream and garnish with plenty of chopped fresh parsley.

Beef Enchiladas

INGREDIENTS

Serves 4

2 pounds chuck steak
1 tablespoon vegetable oil, plus extra
   for frying
1 teaspoon salt
1 teaspoon dried oregano
½ teaspoon ground cumin
1 onion, quartered
2 garlic cloves, crushed
4 cups enchilada sauce
12 corn tortillas
1 cup grated cheese
chopped scallions, to garnish
sour cream, to serve

1 Preheat the oven to 325°F. Place the meat on a sheet of foil and rub it all over with the oil. Sprinkle both sides with the salt, oregano and cumin and rub in well. Add the onion and garlic. Top with another sheet of foil and roll up to seal the edges, leaving room for some steam expansion during cooking.

2 Place in a baking dish and bake for 3 hours, until the meat is tender enough to shred. Remove from the foil and shred the meat using two forks.

3 Stir ½ cup of the enchilada sauce into the beef. Spoon a thin layer of enchilada sauce on the bottom of a rectangular baking dish, or in four individual dishes.

4 Place the remaining sauce in a frying pan and warm gently.

5 Put a ½-inch layer of vegetable oil in a second frying pan and heat until hot but not smoking. With tongs, lower a tortilla into the oil; the temperature is correct if it just sizzles. Cook for 2 seconds, then turn and cook the other side for 2 seconds. Lift out, drain over the pan, and then transfer to the pan with the sauce. Dip in the sauce just to coat both sides.

6 Transfer the softened tortilla immediately to a plate. Spread about 2–3 spoonfuls of the beef mixture down the center of the tortilla. Roll it up and place the filled tortilla seam-side down in the prepared dish. Repeat this process for all the remaining tortillas.

7 Spoon the remaining sauce from the frying pan over the beef enchiladas, spreading it right down to the ends. Sprinkle the grated cheese down the center.

8 Bake the enchiladas until the cheese topping just melts, for about 10–15 minutes. Sprinkle with chopped scallions and serve at once, with sour cream on the side.

COOK'S TIP

For a quicker recipe, use ground beef. Fry in a little oil with chopped onion and garlic, until browned all over. Continue the recipe from step 3.

Red Enchiladas

INGREDIENTS

Serves 6

4 dried *ancho* chilies
1 pound tomatoes, peeled, seeded
  and chopped
1 onion, finely chopped
1 garlic clove, chopped
1 tablespoon chopped fresh cilantro
lard or corn oil for frying
1 cup sour cream
4 chorizo sausages, skinned
  and chopped
18 freshly prepared unbaked
  corn tortillas
2½ cups freshly grated Parmesan
  cheese
salt and freshly ground black pepper

1 Roast the *ancho* chilies in a dry
frying pan over moderate heat for
1–2 minutes, shaking the pan
frequently. When cool, carefully slit the
chilies, remove the stems and seeds,
and tear the pods into pieces. Put in a
bowl, add warm water to cover, and
soak for 20 minutes.

2 Pour the chilies, with a little of
the soaking water, into a food
processor. Add the tomatoes, onion,
garlic and cilantro; purée.

COOK'S TIP

The method of dipping the tortillas first in
sauce, then quickly cooking them in lard
or oil gives the best flavor. If you prefer,
fry the plain tortillas very quickly, then dip
them in the sauce, stuff and roll. There is
not a great loss of flavor, and no spatter.

3 Heat 1 tablespoon of the lard or oil
in a heavy saucepan. Add the purée
and cook gently over medium heat,
stirring, for 3–4 minutes. Season to
taste with salt and pepper and then stir
in the sour cream. Remove the pan
from the heat and set it aside.

4 Heat another tablespoon of the lard
or oil in a small frying pan; sauté
the chorizo for a few minutes, until
lightly browned. Moisten with a little
of the sauce and set the pan aside.

5 Preheat the oven to 350°F. Heat
2 tablespoons of the lard or oil in a
frying pan. Dip a tortilla in the sauce
and add to the pan. Cook for a few
seconds, shaking the pan gently, then
turn over and briefly fry the other side.

6 Slide the tortilla onto a plate, top
with some of the sausage mixture,
and roll up. Pack the prepared tortillas
in a single layer in a baking dish. Pour
the sauce over, sprinkle with Parmesan
and bake for about 20 minutes.

Caribbean Lamb Curry

This popular national dish of Jamaica is known as Curry Goat although goat meat or lamb can be used to make it.

INGREDIENTS

Serves 4–6

2 pounds boned leg of lamb
4 tablespoons curry powder
3 garlic cloves, crushed
1 large onion, chopped
4 thyme sprigs or 1 teaspoon dried thyme
3 bay leaves
1 teaspoon ground allspice
2 tablespoons vegetable oil
4 tablespoons butter or margarine
3¾ cups stock or water
1 fresh hot chili pepper, chopped
cooked rice, to serve
cilantro sprigs, to garnish

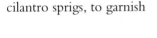

1 Cut the meat into 2-inch cubes, discarding any excess fat and gristle.

3 Melt the butter or margarine in a large heavy saucepan, add the seasoned lamb and fry over a moderate heat for about 10 minutes, turning the meat frequently.

4 Stir in the stock and chili pepper and bring to a boil. Reduce the heat, cover the pan and simmer for 1½ hours, or until the meat is tender. Serve with rice, garnish with cilantro.

2 Place the lamb, curry powder, garlic, onion, thyme, bay leaves, allspice and oil in a large bowl and mix. Marinate in the fridge for at least 3 hours or overnight.

—— COOK'S TIP ——

Try goat, or mutton, if you can and enjoy a robust curry.

Lamb Stew

This stew is known as *Estofado de Carnero* in Mexico. The recipe for this dish has an interesting mix of chilies – the mild, full-flavored *ancho,* and the piquant *jalapeño* which gives extra "bite". The heat of the chilies is mellowed by the addition of ground cinnamon and cloves. Boneless neck fillet is very good for this dish; it is lean, tender, flavorsome and inexpensive.

INGREDIENTS

Serves 4
3 dried *ancho* chilies
2 tablespoons olive oil
1 *jalapeño* pepper, seeded and
  chopped
1 onion, finely chopped
2 garlic cloves, chopped
1 pound tomatoes, peeled and chopped
⅓ cup raisins
¼ teaspoon ground cinnamon
¼ teaspoon ground cloves
2 pounds boneless lamb, cut into
  2-inch cubes
1 cup lamb stock or water
salt and freshly ground black pepper
a few sprigs fresh cilantro, to garnish
cilantro rice, to serve

1 Roast the *ancho* chilies lightly in a dry frying pan over gentle heat to bring out the flavor.

2 Remove the stems, shake out the seeds, tear the pods into pieces, then put them into a bowl. Pour in enough warm water to just cover. Set aside to soak for 30 minutes.

3 Heat the olive oil in a frying pan and sauté the *jalapeño* together with the onion and garlic until the onion is tender.

4 Add the chopped tomatoes to the pan and cook until the mixture is thick and well blended. Stir in the raisins, ground cinnamon and cloves, and season to taste with salt and ground black pepper. Transfer the mixture to a flameproof casserole.

5 Tip the *ancho* chilies and their soaking water into a food processor and process to a smooth purée. Add the chili purée to the tomato mixture in the casserole.

6 Add the lamb to the casserole, stir to mix and pour in enough of the lamb stock to just cover the meat.

7 Bring to a simmer, then cover the casserole and cook over low heat for about 2 hours or until the lamb is tender. Garnish with fresh cilantro and serve with cilantro rice.

COOK'S TIP

To make cilantro rice, simply heat 2 tablespoons corn oil in a large frying pan and gently cook 1 finely chopped onion for about 8 minutes, or until soft but not brown. Add enough cooked long-grain rice to serve four, and stir gently over medium-low heat until heated through. Sprinkle with 2–3 tablespoons chopped fresh cilantro and stir in thoroughly.

Sweet and Sour Pork

INGREDIENTS

Serves 4

12 ounces lean pork
¼ teaspoon salt and ½ teaspoon ground
  Szechuan peppercorns
1 tablespoon Chinese rice wine
4 ounces bamboo shoots
2 tablespoons all-purpose flour
1 egg, lightly beaten
1 tablespoon vegetable oil, plus extra
  for frying
1 garlic clove, finely chopped
1 scallion, cut into short sections
1 small green bell pepper, diced finely
1 fresh red chili, seeded and shredded
1 tablespoon light soy sauce
2 tablespoons light brown sugar
3 tablespoons rice vinegar
1 tablespoon tomato paste
½ cup stock

1 Using a sharp knife, cut the lean pork into small bite-size cubes. Marinate with the salt, ground peppercorns and Chinese wine for about 15–20 minutes.

2 Cut the bamboo shoots into small cubes about the same size as the pork pieces.

3 Dust the pork with flour, dip in the beaten egg, and coat with more flour. Deep-fry in moderately hot oil for 3–4 minutes, stirring to separate the pieces. Remove.

4 Reheat the oil, add the pork and bamboo shoots, and fry for 1 minute, or until golden. Drain.

5 Heat 1 tablespoon oil and add the garlic, scallion, bell pepper and chili. Stir-fry for 30–40 seconds, then add the seasonings with the stock. Bring to a boil, then add the pork and bamboo shoots.

Lamb Tagine with Cilantro and Spices

This is a version of a Moroccan-style tagine in which chops or cutlets are sprinkled with spices and either marinated for a few hours or cooked straightaway.

INGREDIENTS

Serves 4

4 lamb chops or cutlets
2 garlic cloves, crushed
pinch of saffron strands
½ teaspoon ground cinnamon, plus extra to garnish
½ teaspoon ground ginger
1 tablespoon chopped fresh cilantro
1 tablespoon chopped fresh parsley
1 onion, finely chopped
3 tablespoons olive oil
1¼ cups lamb stock
½ cup blanched almonds, to garnish
1 teaspoon sugar
salt and freshly ground black pepper

1 Season the lamb with the garlic, saffron, cinnamon, ginger and a little salt and black pepper. Place on a large plate and sprinkle with the cilantro, parsley and onion. Cover loosely and set aside in the fridge for a few hours to marinate.

2 Heat the oil in a large frying pan, over a moderate heat. Add the marinated lamb and all the herbs and onion from the dish.

3 Fry for 1–2 minutes, turning once, then add the stock, bring to a boil and simmer gently for 30 minutes, turning the chops once.

4 Meanwhile, heat a small frying pan over a moderate heat, add the almonds and dry fry until golden, shaking the pan occasionally to make sure they color evenly. Transfer to a bowl and set aside.

5 Transfer the chops to a serving plate and keep warm. Increase the heat under the pan and boil the sauce until reduced by about half. Stir in the sugar. Pour the sauce over the chops and sprinkle with the fried almonds and a little extra ground cinnamon.

COOK'S TIP

Lamb tagine is a fragrant dish, originating in North Africa. It is traditionally made in a cooking dish known as a tagine, from which it takes its name. This dish consists of a shallow pot with a conical lid. It has a narrow opening to let steam escape, while retaining the flavor.

Khara Masala Lamb

Whole spices are used in this curry so you should warn the diners of their presence in advance! It is delicious when served with freshly baked naan bread or a rice accompaniment. This dish is best made with good-quality spring lamb.

INGREDIENTS

Serves 4

5 tablespoons corn oil
2 onions, chopped
1 teaspoon shredded ginger
1 teaspoon sliced garlic
6 whole dried red chilies
3 cardamom pods
2 cinnamon sticks
6 black peppercorns
3 cloves
½ teaspoon salt
1 pound boned leg of lamb, cubed
2½ cups water
2 fresh green chilies, sliced
2 tablespoons chopped fresh cilantro

1 Heat the oil in a large saucepan. Lower the heat slightly and fry the onions until they are lightly browned.

2 Add half the ginger and half the garlic and stir well.

3 Throw in half the red chilies, the cardamoms, cinnamon, peppercorns, cloves and salt.

4 Add the lamb and fry over medium heat. Stir continuously with a semi-circular movement, using a wooden spoon to scrape the bottom of the pan. Continue in this way for about 5 minutes.

5 Pour in the water, cover with a lid and cook over medium-low heat for 35–40 minutes, or until the water has evaporated and the meat is tender.

6 Add the rest of the shredded ginger, sliced garlic and the whole dried red chilies, along with the sliced fresh green chilies and the fresh chopped cilantro.

COOK'S TIP

The action of stirring the meat and spices together using a semi-circular motion, as described in step 4, is called bhoono-ing. It makes sure that the meat becomes well-coated and combined with the spice mixture before the cooking liquid is added.

7 Continue to stir over the heat until you see some free oil on the sides of the pan. Transfer to a serving dish and serve immediately.

Deep-fried Spareribs with Spicy Salt and Pepper

If you want these spareribs to be hotter, just increase the amount of chili sauce.

INGREDIENTS

Serves 4–6
10–12 finger ribs, in total about
   1½ pounds, with excess fat and
   gristle trimmed
about 2–3 tablespoons flour
vegetable oil, for deep-frying

For the marinade
1 garlic clove, crushed and chopped
1 tablespoon light brown sugar
1 tablespoon dark soy sauce
2 tablespoons Chinese rice wine or
   dry sherry
½ teaspoon chili sauce
few drops sesame oil

1 Chop each rib into 3–4 pieces. Combine all the marinade ingredients in a bowl, add the spareribs and marinate for at least 2–3 hours.

2 Coat the spareribs with flour and deep-fry them in medium-hot oil for 4–5 minutes, stirring to separate. Remove and drain.

3 Heat the oil to high and deep-fry the spareribs once more for about 1 minute, or until the color is an even dark brown. Remove and drain, then serve hot.

> ——— SPICY SALT AND PEPPER ———
>
> To make Spicy Salt and Pepper, mix 1 tablespoon salt with 2 teaspoons ground Szechuan peppercorns and 1 teaspoon five-spice powder. Heat together in a preheated dry pan for about 2 minutes over low heat, stirring constantly. This quantity is sufficient for at least six servings.

Pork with Chilies and Pineapple

INGREDIENTS

Serves 6

2 tablespoons corn oil
2 pounds boneless pork shoulder
  or loin, cut into 2-inch cubes
1 onion, finely chopped
1 large red bell pepper, seeded
  and finely chopped
1 or more *jalapeño* peppers, seeded and
  finely chopped
1 pound fresh pineapple chunks
8 fresh mint leaves, chopped
1 cup chicken stock
salt and freshly ground black pepper
fresh mint sprig, to garnish
rice, to serve

1 Heat the oil in a large frying pan and sauté the pork cubes in batches until lightly browned. Transfer the pork to a flameproof casserole, leaving the oil behind in the pan.

2 Add the onion, red pepper and the *jalapeño* to the oil remaining in the pan. Sauté until the onion is tender, then add to the casserole with the pineapple. Stir to combine.

3 Add the mint, then cover and simmer gently for about 2 hours, or until the pork is tender. Garnish with fresh mint and serve with rice.

COOK'S TIP

If fresh pineapple is not available, use pineapple canned in its own juice.

Mole Poblano de Guajolote

Mole Poblano de Guajolote is *the* great festive dish of Mexico. It is served at any special occasion, be it a birthday, wedding, or family get-together. Rice, beans, tortillas and guacamole are the traditional accompaniments.

INGREDIENTS

Serves 6–8

6–8 pounds turkey, cut into
   serving pieces
1 onion, chopped
1 garlic clove, chopped
salt
6 tablespoons lard or corn oil
fresh cilantro and 2 tablespoons toasted
   sesame seeds, to garnish

For the sauce
6 dried *ancho* chilies
4 dried *pasilla* chilies
4 dried *mulato* chilies
1 drained canned *chipotle* chili, seeded
   and chopped (optional)
2 onions, chopped
2 garlic cloves, chopped
1 pound tomatoes, peeled
   and chopped
1 stale tortilla, torn into pieces
⅓ cup raisins
1 cup ground almonds
3 tablespoons sesame seeds, ground
½ tsp coriander seeds, ground
1 teaspoon ground cinnamon
½ teaspoon ground anise
¼ teaspoon ground black peppercorns
4 tablespoons lard or corn oil
1½ ounces unsweetened chocolate,
   broken into squares
1 tablespoon sugar
salt and freshly ground pepper

COOK'S TIP

Roasting the dried chilies lightly, taking care not to burn them, brings out the flavor and is worth the extra effort.

---

1 Put the turkey pieces into a saucepan or flameproof casserole large enough to hold them in one layer comfortably. Add the onion and garlic, and enough cold water to cover. Season with salt, bring to a gentle simmer, cover and cook for about 1 hour or until the turkey is tender.

2 Meanwhile, put the *ancho, pasilla* and *mulato* chilies in a dry frying pan over gentle heat and roast them for a few minutes, shaking the pan frequently. Remove the stems and shake out the seeds. Tear the pods into pieces and put these into a small bowl. Add sufficient warm water to just cover and soak, turning from time to time, for 30 minutes, or until soft.

3 Lift out the turkey pieces and pat dry with paper towels. Reserve the stock in a measuring jug. Heat the lard in a large heavy frying pan and sauté the turkey pieces until lightly browned all over. Transfer to a plate and set aside. Reserve any oil left in the frying pan.

4 Transfer the chilies, along with the water in which they have been soaked, into a food processor. Add the *chipotle* chili, if using, with the onions, garlic, tomatoes, tortilla, raisins, ground almonds and spices. Process to a purée. Do this in batches, if necessary.

5 Add the lard to the fat remaining in the frying pan used for sautéing the turkey. Heat the mixture, then add the chili and spice paste. Cook, stirring, for 5 minutes.

6 Transfer the mixture to the pan or casserole in which the turkey was originally cooked. Stir in 2 cups of the turkey stock (make up the difference with water if necessary). Add the chocolate and season with salt and pepper. Cook over low heat until the chocolate has melted. Stir in the sugar. Add the turkey and more stock if needed. Cover the pan and simmer very gently for 30 minutes. Serve, garnished with fresh cilantro and sprinkled with the sesame seeds.

Spicy Meatballs

Serve these Indonesian meatballs with a sambal or a spicy sauce.

INGREDIENTS

Makes 24
1 large onion, roughly chopped
1–2 fresh red chilies, seeded
  and chopped
2 garlic cloves, crushed
½-inch cube shrimp paste
1 tablespoon coriander seeds
1 teaspoon cumin seeds
1 pound lean ground beef
2 teaspoons dark soy sauce
1 teaspoon dark brown sugar
juice of ½ lemon
a little beaten egg
oil for shallow-frying
salt and freshly ground black pepper
fresh cilantro sprigs, to garnish

1 Put the onions, chilies, garlic and shrimp paste in a food processor. Process but do not over-chop or the onion will become too wet and spoil the consistency of the meatballs. Dry-fry the coriander and cumin seeds in a preheated pan for about 1 minute, to release the aroma. Do not brown. Grind with a pestle and mortar.

2 Put the meat in a large bowl. Stir in the onion mixture. Add the ground coriander and cumin, soy sauce, seasoning, sugar and lemon juice. Bind with a little beaten egg and shape into small, even-size balls.

3 Chill the meatballs briefly to firm them, if necessary. Fry in shallow oil, turning often, until cooked through and browned. This will take 4–5 minutes, depending on their size.

4 Remove from the pan, drain on paper towels and serve, garnished with cilantro sprigs.

Beef and Eggplant Curry

INGREDIENTS

Serves 6

½ cup sunflower oil
2 onions, thinly sliced
1 inch fresh ginger root, sliced and
    cut in matchsticks
1 garlic clove, crushed
2 fresh red chilies, seeded and very
    finely sliced
1 inch fresh turmeric, peeled and
    crushed, or 1 teaspoon
    ground turmeric
1 lemon grass stem, lower part finely
    sliced, top bruised
1½ pounds braising steak, cut in even-
    size strips
14 fluid-ounce can coconut milk
1¼ cups water
1 eggplant, sliced and patted dry
1 teaspoon tamarind pulp, soaked in
    4 tablespoons warm water
salt and freshly ground black pepper
finely sliced chili and deep-fried
    onions, to garnish
boiled rice, to serve

1 Heat half the oil and fry the
onions, ginger and garlic until they
give off a rich aroma. Add the chilies,
turmeric and the lower part of the
lemon grass. Push to one side and then
turn up the heat and add the steak,
stirring until the meat changes color.

> ───── COOK'S TIP ─────
>
> If you want to make this curry, *Gulai
> Terung Dengan Daging,* ahead, prepare to
> the end of step 2 and finish later.

2 Add the coconut milk, water,
lemon grass top and seasoning to
taste. Cover and simmer gently for
1½ hours, or until the meat is tender.

3 Towards the end of the cooking
time heat the remaining oil in a
frying pan. Fry the eggplant slices until
brown on both sides.

4 Add the browned eggplant slices to
the beef curry and cook for a
further 15 minutes. Stir gently from
time to time. Strain the tamarind and
stir the juice into the curry. Taste and
adjust the seasoning. Put into a warm
serving dish. Garnish with the sliced
chili and deep-fried onions and serve
with boiled rice.

Spicy Fried Chicken

This crispy chicken is superb hot or cold. Served with a salad or vegetables, it makes a delicious lunch and is ideal for picnics or snacks too.

INGREDIENTS

Serves 4–6
4 chicken drumsticks
4 chicken thighs
2 teaspoons curry powder
½ teaspoon garlic powder
½ teaspoon ground black pepper
½ teaspoon paprika
1¼ cups milk
oil, for deep frying
4 tablespoons all-purpose flour
salt
lettuce leaves, to serve

1 Place the chicken pieces in a large bowl and sprinkle with the curry powder, garlic powder, black pepper, paprika and salt. Rub the spices well into the chicken, then cover and let marinate in a cool place for at least 2 hours, or overnight in the fridge.

2 Preheat the oven to 350°F. Pour enough milk into the bowl to cover the chicken and leave to stand for a further 15 minutes.

3 Heat the oil in a large saucepan or deep-fat fryer and sprinkle the flour onto a plate. Shake off excess milk, dip each piece of chicken in flour and fry two or three pieces at a time until golden, but not cooked. Continue until all the chicken pieces are fried.

4 Remove with a slotted spoon, place the chicken pieces on a baking sheet, and bake for about 30 minutes. Serve hot or cold with lettuce leaves.

Spicy Chicken with Coconut

Traditionally, the chicken pieces for this Indonesian dish would be part-cooked by frying, but roasting in the oven is just as successful. This recipe is unusual in that it does not contain any chilies or turmeric, but galangal, lemon grass, cilantro and lime leaves add a deliciously spicy flavor.

INGREDIENTS

3–3½-pound chicken or 4 chicken
   quarters
4 garlic cloves
1 onion, sliced
4 macadamia nuts or 8 almonds
1 tablespoon coriander seeds, dry-fried,
   or 1 teaspoon ground coriander
3 tablespoons oil
1-inch piece fresh galangal, peeled
   and bruised
2 lemon grass stems, fleshy part bruised
3 lime leaves
2 bay leaves
1 teaspoon sugar
600ml/1 pint/2½ cups coconut milk
salt
boiled rice and deep-fried onions, to
   serve

1 Preheat the oven to 375°F. Cut the chicken into four or eight pieces. Season with salt. Put in an oiled roasting pan and cook in the oven for 25–30 minutes. Meanwhile, prepare the sauce.

2 Grind the garlic, onion, nuts and coriander to a fine paste in a food processor or with a mortar and pestle. Heat the oil and fry the paste to bring out the flavor. Do not allow it to brown.

3 Add the part-cooked chicken pieces to a wok together with the *laos*, lemon grass, lime and bay leaves, sugar, coconut milk and salt to taste. Mix well to coat in the sauce.

4 Bring to a boil and then reduce the heat and simmer gently for 30–40 minutes, uncovered, until the chicken is tender and the coconut sauce is reduced and thickened. Stir the mixture occasionally during cooking.

5 Just before serving, remove the bruised galangal and lemon grass. Serve with boiled rice sprinkled with crisp deep-fried onions.

Crispy and Aromatic Duck

As this dish is often served with pancakes, scallions, cucumber and duck sauce (a sweet bean paste), many people mistake it for Peking Duck. This recipe, however, uses a different cooking method. The result is just as crispy but the delightful aroma makes this dish particularly distinctive. Plum sauce may be substituted for the duck sauce.

INGREDIENTS

Serves 6–8

1 oven-ready duckling,
    about 5–5¼ pounds
2 teaspoons salt
5–6 whole star anise
1 tablespoon Szechuan peppercorns
1 teaspoon cloves
2–3 cinnamon sticks
3–4 scallions
3–4 slices fresh ginger, unpeeled
5–6 tablespoons Chinese rice wine
    or dry sherry
vegetable oil, for deep-frying
lettuce leaves, to garnish

To serve

Chinese pancakes
duck sauce
scallions, shredded
cucumber, diced

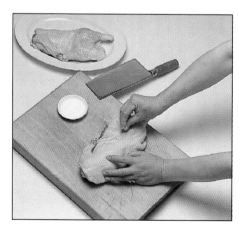

1 Remove the wings from the duck and split the body in half down the backbone.

2 Rub salt all over the two duck halves, taking care to work it all in thoroughly.

3 Marinate the duck in a dish with the spices, scallions, fresh ginger and rice wine or dry sherry for at least 4–6 hours.

4 Vigorously steam the duck with the marinade for 3–4 hours (or for longer if possible). Carefully remove the steamed duck from the cooking liquid and let cool for at least 5–6 hours. The duck must be cold and dry or the skin will not be crispy.

5 Heat the vegetable oil in a wok until it is just smoking, then place the duck pieces in the oil, skin-side down. Deep-fry the duck for about 5–6 minutes, or until it becomes crisp and brown. Turn the duck just once at the very last moment.

6 Remove the fried duck, drain it well and place it on a bed of lettuce leaves.

7 To serve, scrape the meat off the bone and wrap a portion in each pancake with a little duck sauce, shredded scallions and cucumber. Eat with your fingers.

COOK'S TIP

Small pancakes suitable for this dish can be found in most Chinese stores. They can be frozen and will keep for up to 3 months in the freezer.

Barbecued Jerk Chicken

Jerk refers to the blend of herb and spice seasoning rubbed into meat, before it is roasted over charcoal sprinkled with pimiento berries. In Jamaica, jerk seasoning was originally used only for pork, but jerk chicken is equally good.

INGREDIENTS

Serves 4
8 chicken pieces

For the marinade
1 teaspoon ground allspice
1 teaspoon ground cinnamon
1 teaspoon dried thyme
¼ teaspoon freshly grated nutmeg
2 teaspoons raw sugar
2 garlic cloves, crushed
1 tablespoon finely chopped onion
1 tablespoon chopped scallion
1 tablespoon vinegar
2 tablespoons oil
1 tablespoon lime juice
1 hot chili pepper, chopped
salt and freshly ground black pepper
lettuce leaves, to serve

1 Combine all the marinade ingredients in a small bowl. Using a fork, mash them together well to make a thick paste.

2 Lay the chicken pieces on a plate or board and make several lengthwise slits in the flesh. Rub the seasoning all over the chicken and into the slits.

3 Place the chicken pieces in a dish, cover with plastic wrap and let marinate overnight in the fridge.

4 Shake off any excess seasoning from the chicken. Brush with oil and either place on a baking sheet or on a barbecue grill if barbecuing. Cook under a preheated broiler for 45 minutes, turning often. Or, if barbecuing, light the coals and when ready, cook over the coals for 30 minutes, turning often. Serve hot with lettuce leaves.

— COOK'S TIP —

The flavor is best if you marinate the chicken overnight. Sprinkle the charcoal with aromatic herbs such as bay leaves for even more flavor.

Blackened Hot Chicken Breasts

INGREDIENTS

Serves 6

6 skinless, boneless chicken breasts
6 tablespoons butter or margarine
1 teaspoon garlic powder
2 teaspoons onion powder
1 teaspoon cayenne pepper
2 teaspoons sweet paprika
1½ teaspoons salt
½ teaspoon white pepper
1 teaspoon ground black pepper
¼ teaspoon ground cumin
1 teaspoon dried thyme

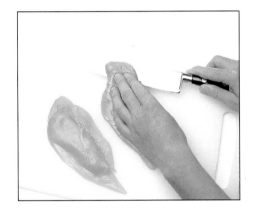

1 Slice each chicken breast piece in half horizontally, making two pieces of about the same thickness. Flatten slightly with the heel of your hand.

2 Melt the butter or margarine in a small saucepan.

4 Heat a large, heavy frying pan over high heat until a drop of water sprinkled on the surface sizzles. This will take 5–8 minutes.

5 Drizzle 1 teaspoon melted butter on each chicken piece. Place them in the pan in an even layer, two or three at a time. Cook for 2–3 minutes until the underside begins to blacken. Turn and cook the other side for 2–3 minutes more. Serve hot.

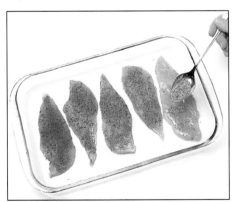

3 Combine all the remaining ingredients in a shallow bowl and stir to blend well. Brush the chicken pieces on both sides with melted butter or margarine, then sprinkle evenly with the seasoning mixture.

Hot Chicken Curry

This curry has a nice thick sauce, and using red and green bell peppers gives it extra color. It can be served with either whole wheat chapatis or boiled rice.

INGREDIENTS

Serves 4

2 tablespoons corn oil
¼ teaspoon fenugreek seeds
¼ teaspoon onion seeds
2 onions, chopped
½ teaspoon garlic pulp
½ teaspoon ginger pulp
1 teaspoon ground coriander
1 teaspoon chili powder
1 teaspoon salt
1¾ cups canned tomatoes
2 tablespoons lemon juice
2½ cups chicken, skinned, boned and cubed
2 tablespoons chopped fresh cilantro
3 fresh green chilies, chopped
½ red bell pepper, cut into chunks
½ green bell pepper, cut into chunks
fresh cilantro sprigs

1 In a medium saucepan, heat the oil and fry the fenugreek and onion seeds until they turn a shade darker. Add the chopped onions, garlic and ginger and fry for about 5 minutes until the onions turn golden brown. Turn the heat to very low.

2 Meanwhile, in a separate bowl, mix together the ground coriander, chili powder, salt, canned tomatoes and lemon juice.

3 Pour this mixture into the saucepan and turn up the heat to medium. Stir-fry for about 3 minutes.

4 Add the chicken pieces and stir-fry for 5–7 minutes.

5 Add the fresh cilantro, green chilies and the red and green bell peppers. Lower the heat, cover the saucepan and let this simmer for about 10 minutes until the chicken is cooked.

6 Serve hot, garnished with fresh cilantro sprigs.

COOK'S TIP

For a milder version of this delicious chicken curry, simply omit some of the fresh green chilies.

Spatchcocked Deviled Poussins

English mustard adds a hot touch to the spice paste used in this tasty recipe.

INGREDIENTS

Serves 4

1 tablespoon English mustard powder
1 tablespoon paprika
1 tablespoon ground cumin
4 teaspoons tomato ketchup
1 tablespoon lemon juice
5 tablespoons butter, melted
4 poussins, about 1 pound each
salt

1 In a mixing bowl, combine the English mustard, paprika, ground cumin, tomato ketchup, lemon juice and salt. Mix together until smooth, then gradually stir in the melted butter until incorporated.

2 Using game shears or a strong pair of kitchen scissors, split each poussin along one side of the backbone, then cut down the other side of the backbone to remove it.

3 Open out a poussin, skin-side uppermost, then press down firmly with the heel of your hand. Pass a long skewer through one leg and out through the other to secure the bird open and flat. Repeat with the remaining birds.

4 Spread the spicy mustard mixture evenly over the skin of each of the poussins. Cover them loosely and let stand in a cool place for at least 2 hours. Preheat the broiler.

5 Place the prepared poussins, skin-side uppermost, on a broiler rack and broil them for about 12 minutes. Turn the birds over, baste with any juices in the pan, and cook for 7 minutes more, until all the juices run clear.

COOK'S TIP

Spatchcocked poussins cook very well on the barbecue. Make sure that the coals are very hot, then cook the birds for about 15–20 minutes, turning and basting them frequently as they cook.

Bon-bon Chicken with Spicy Sesame

In this recipe, the chicken meat is tenderized by being beaten with a stick (called a "bon" in Chinese) – hence the name for this very popular Szechuan dish.

INGREDIENTS

Serves 6–8

1 whole chicken, about 2¼ pounds
5 cups water
1 tablespoon sesame oil
shredded cucumber, to garnish

For the sauce

2 tablespoons light soy sauce
1 teaspoon sugar
1 tablespoon finely chopped scallions
1 teaspoon red chili oil
½ teaspoon ground Szechuan
   peppercorns
1 teaspoon white sesame seeds
2 tablespoons sesame paste, or
   2 tablespoons peanut butter creamed
   with a little sesame oil

1 Clean the chicken well. In a wok or saucepan bring the water to a rolling boil, add the chicken, reduce the heat and cook under cover for 40–45 minutes. Remove the chicken and immerse in cold water to cool.

2 After at least 1 hour, remove the chicken and drain; dry well with paper towels and brush with sesame oil. Carve the meat from the legs, wings and breast and pull the meat off the rest of the bones.

3 On a flat surface, pound the meat with a rolling pin, then tear the meat into shreds with your fingers.

4 Place the meat in a dish with the shredded cucumber around the edge. In a bowl, mix together all the sauce ingredients, keeping a few scallions to garnish. Pour over the chicken and serve.

COOK'S TIP

To make chili oil, slit and blanch chilies, pack into sterilized jars and fill with oil. Let stand for 2 weeks.

Chicken Sauce Piquante

Red chili peppers add heat to this Cajun recipe. Sauce Piquante is commonly used in lots of recipes to liven up meat and fish and give meals a spicy taste.

INGREDIENTS

Serves 4

4 chicken legs or 2 legs and 2 breasts
5 tablespoons oil
½ cup all-purpose flour
1 onion, chopped
2 celery stalks, sliced
1 green bell pepper, seeded and diced
2 garlic cloves, crushed
1 bay leaf
½ teaspoon dried thyme
½ teaspoon dried oregano
1–2 red chili peppers, seeded and finely chopped
14-ounce can tomatoes, chopped, with their juice
1¼ cups chicken stock
salt and ground black pepper
watercress, to garnish
boiled potatoes, to serve

— COOK'S TIP —

If you prefer to err on the side of caution with chili heat, use just 1 chili pepper and hot up the seasoning at the end with a dash or two of Tabasco sauce.

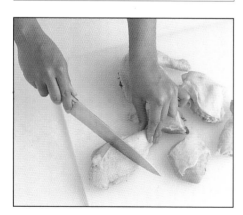

1 Halve the chicken legs through the joint, or the breasts across the middle, to give eight pieces.

2 In a heavy frying pan, fry the chicken pieces in the oil until brown on all sides, lifting them out and setting them aside as they are done.

3 Strain the oil from the pan into a heavy flameproof casserole. Heat it and stir in the flour. Stir constantly over low heat until the roux is the color of peanut butter.

4 As soon as the roux reaches the right stage, add the onion, celery and bell pepper and stir over the heat for 2–3 minutes.

5 Add the garlic, bay leaf, thyme, oregano and chili pepper(s). Stir for 1 minute, then turn down the heat and stir in the tomatoes with their juice.

6 Return the casserole to the heat and gradually stir in the stock. Add the chicken pieces, cover and let simmer for 45 minutes, until the chicken is tender.

7 If there is too much sauce or it is too runny, remove the lid for the last 10–15 minutes of the cooking time and raise the heat a little.

8 Check the seasoning and serve garnished with watercress and accompanied by boiled potatoes, or perhaps rice or pasta, and a green vegetable or salad of your choice.

— VARIATION —

Any kind of meat, poultry or fish can be served with Sauce Piquante. Just cook the meat or fish first, then serve it with plenty of the sauce.

Tandoori Chicken

INGREDIENTS

Serves 4

4 chicken quarters
³/₄ cup plain low-fat yogurt
1 teaspoon garam masala
1 teaspoon ginger pulp
1 teaspoon garlic pulp
1½ teaspoons chili powder
¼ teaspoon turmeric
1 teaspoon ground coriander
1 tablespoon lemon juice
1 teaspoon salt
few drops red food coloring
2 tablespoons corn oil
mixed salad leaves, lime wedges and
    1 tomato, quartered, to garnish

1 Skin the chicken quarters, rinse under cold water then pat dry on kitchen paper. Make two slits into the flesh of each piece, place them in a large ovenproof dish and set aside while making the tandoori paste.

2 Mix together the yogurt, garam masala, ginger, garlic, chili powder, turmeric, ground coriander, lemon juice, salt, red coloring and oil, and beat so that all the ingredients are well mixed together.

3 Cover the chicken quarters with the spice mixture and let marinate for about 3 hours.

4 Preheat the oven to 475°F. Transfer the chicken pieces to an ovenproof dish.

5 Bake in the preheated oven for 20–25 minutes, or until the chicken is cooked right through and browned on top.

6 Remove from the oven, transfer to a serving dish and garnish with the salad leaves, lime and tomato.

COOK'S TIP

The red food coloring gives this dish its traditional appearance, but it can be omitted if wished.

Spicy Masala Chicken

These chicken pieces are broiled and have a sweet-and-sour taste. They can be served cold with a salad and rice, or hot with Masala Mashed Potatoes.

INGREDIENTS

Serves 6

12 chicken thighs
6 tablespoons lemon juice
1 teaspoon ginger pulp
1 teaspoon garlic pulp
1 teaspoon crushed dried red chilies
1 teaspoon salt
1 teaspoon brown sugar
2 tablespoons honey
2 tablespoons chopped fresh cilantro
1 fresh green chili, finely chopped
2 tablespoons vegetable oil
fresh cilantro sprigs, to garnish

COOK'S TIP

Masala refers to the blend of spices used in this dish. The amounts can be varied according to taste.

1 Prick all the chicken thighs with a fork. Rinse them, pat dry and set aside in a bowl.

2 In a large mixing bowl, mix together the lemon juice, ginger, garlic, crushed dried red chilies, salt, sugar and honey.

3 Transfer the chicken thighs to the spice mixture and coat well. Set aside for about 45 minutes.

4 Preheat the broiler to medium. Add the fresh cilantro and chopped green chili to the chicken thighs and place them in a flameproof dish.

5 Pour any remaining marinade over the chicken and baste with the oil, using a pastry brush.

6 Broil the chicken thighs under the broiler for 15–20 minutes, turning and basting occasionally, until cooked through and browned.

7 Transfer to a serving dish and garnish with the fresh cilantro sprigs.

HOT AND VIBRANT VEGETABLES AND SALADS

Vegetables have a mild flavor which makes them perfect partners for assertive spices and hot chilies. Potatoes will never seem bland again after Potatoes with Red Chilies – this dish is for serious chili addicts. Have fun with Mexican recipes such as Black Bean Burritos and Frijoles, which is simply cooked beans spiked with serrano chilies.

Szechuan Spicy Beancurd

The ground beef can be omitted in this dish to create a purely vegetarian meal.

INGREDIENTS

Serves 4

1 package beancurd
1 leek
4 ounces ground beef
3 tablespoons vegetable oil
1 tablespoon black bean sauce
1 tablespoon light soy sauce
1 teaspoon chili bean sauce
1 tablespoon Chinese rice wine
  or dry sherry
about 3–4 tablespoons vegetable stock
2 teaspoons cornstarch paste
ground Szechuan peppercorns, to taste
few drops sesame oil

1 Cut the beancurd into ½-inch cubes and blanch them in a pan of boiling water for about 2–3 minutes until they harden. Remove the cubes with a slotted spoon and drain on paper towels. Cut the leek into short sections.

2 Stir-fry the ground beef in oil until the color changes, then add the chopped leek and black bean sauce. Add the beancurd with the soy sauce, chili bean sauce and wine or sherry. Stir gently for 1 minute.

3 Add the vegetable stock, bring to a boil and braise the mixture for about 2–3 minutes.

4 Thicken the spicy sauce with the cornstarch paste, season with the ground Szechuan peppercorns and sprinkle with some drops of sesame oil. Serve immediately.

Potatoes with Red Chilies

The quantity of red chilies used in this potato dish may be too fiery for some palates. If you would prefer to make a milder version, you could either seed the red chilies, use fewer of them or just substitute them with a chopped red bell pepper.

INGREDIENTS

Serves 4

12–14 baby new potatoes, halved
2 tablespoons vegetable oil
½ teaspoon crushed dried red chilies
½ teaspoon white cumin seeds
½ teaspoon fennel seeds
½ teaspoon crushed coriander seeds
1 tablespoon salt
1 onion, sliced
1–4 fresh red chilies, halved lengthwise
1 tablespoon chopped fresh cilantro

— COOK'S TIP —

Make sure you serve this fiery dish with plenty of cooling yogurt or raita, and some naan or chapatis.

1 Boil the halved baby potatoes in a saucepan of salted water until they are soft but still firm to the touch. Remove them from the heat and drain off the water.

2 In a deep frying pan, heat the oil, then turn down the heat to medium. Add the crushed chilies, cumin, fennel and coriander seeds and salt and fry for 30–40 seconds.

3 Add the sliced onion and fry until it is golden brown. Then add the potatoes, fresh red chilies and chopped fresh cilantro.

4 Cover and cook for 5–7 minutes over very low heat. Serve hot.

Green Chili Dhal

This dhal (Tarka Dhal) is probably the most popular of lentil dishes and is found in most Indian and Pakistani restaurants.

INGREDIENTS

Serves 4

½ cup masoor dhal (split red lentils)
¼ cup moong dhal (small split
   yellow lentils)
2½ cups water
1 teaspoon ginger pulp
1 teaspoon garlic pulp
¼ teaspoon turmeric
2 fresh green chilies, chopped
1½ teaspoons salt

For the tarka

2 tablespoons oil
1 onion, sliced
¼ teaspoon mixed mustard and
   onion seeds
4 dried red chilies
1 tomato, sliced

To garnish

1 tablespoon chopped fresh cilantro
1–2 fresh green chilies, seeded
   and sliced
1 tablespoon chopped fresh mint

1 Pick over the lentils for any stones before washing them.

2 Boil the lentils in the water with the ginger, garlic, turmeric and chopped green chilies for about 15–20 minutes until soft.

3 Mash the lentil mixture down. The consistency of the mashed lentils should be similar to that of a creamy chicken soup.

4 If the mixture looks too dry, just add some more water. Season with the salt.

5 To prepare the tarka, heat the oil, and fry the onion with the mustard and onion seeds, dried red chilies and sliced tomato for 2 minutes.

6 Pour the tarka over the dhal and garnish with fresh cilantro, green chilies and mint.

--- COOK'S TIP ---

Dried red chilies are available in many different sizes. If the ones you have are large, or if you want a less spicy flavor, reduce the quantity specified to 1–2.

Frijoles

INGREDIENTS

Serves 6–8

1¼–1½ cups dried red kidney, pinto or black beans, rinsed and picked over
2 onions, finely chopped
2 garlic cloves, chopped
1 bay leaf
1 or more *serrano* chilies (small fresh hot green chilies)
2 tablespoons corn oil
2 tomatoes, peeled, seeded and chopped
salt
sprigs of fresh bay leaves, to garnish

COOK'S TIP

In the Yucatán, black haricot beans are cooked with the Mexican herb *epazote*.

---

1 Put the beans into a pan and add cold water to cover by 1 inch.

2 Add half the onion, half the garlic, the bay leaf and the chili(es). Bring to a boil and boil vigorously for about 10 minutes. Put the beans and liquid into a large saucepan, cover and cook over low heat for 30 minutes. Add boiling water if the beans start to become dry.

3 When the beans begin to wrinkle, add 1 tablespoon of the corn oil and cook for another 30 minutes or until the beans are tender. Add salt to taste and cook for 30 minutes more, but do not add any more water.

4 Remove the beans from the heat. Heat the remaining oil in a small frying pan and sauté the remaining onion and garlic until the onion is soft. Add the tomatoes and cook for a few minutes more.

5 Spoon 3 tablespoons of the beans out of the pot or pan and add them to the tomato mixture. Mash to a paste. Stir this into the beans to thicken the liquid. Cook for just long enough to heat through, if necessary. Serve the beans in small bowls and garnish with sprigs of fresh bay leaves.

Black Bean Burritos

INGREDIENTS

Serves 4

1 cup dried black beans, soaked
   overnight and drained
1 bay leaf
3 tablespoons sea salt
1 small red onion, chopped
2 cups grated cheese
3 tablespoons chopped pickled jalapeños
1 tablespoon chopped fresh cilantro
3 cups tomato salsa
8 flour tortillas
diced avocado, to serve

1 Place the beans in a large pan. Add cold water to cover and the bay leaf. Bring to a boil, then cover, and simmer for 30 minutes. Add the salt and continue simmering for about 30 minutes until tender. Drain and cool slightly. Discard the bay leaf.

2 Preheat the oven to 350°F. Grease a rectangular baking dish with vegetable oil.

3 In a mixing bowl, combine the drained beans, onion, half the cheese, the jalapeños, cilantro and 1 cup tomato salsa. Stir to blend, and taste for seasoning.

4 Place one tortilla on a clean work surface. Spread a large spoonful of the filling down the middle, then roll it up to enclose the filling completely. Place the burrito in the prepared dish, seam-side down. Repeat this process with the remaining tortillas until the dish is full.

5 Sprinkle the remaining cheese over the burritos, in an even line right down the middle. Bake in the oven for about 15 minutes, or until the cheese melts completely.

6 Serve the bean burritos immediately, with diced avocado and the remaining salsa.

Chili Zucchini

Calabacitas is an extremely easy recipe to make. If the cooking time seems unduly long, this is because the acid present in the tomatoes slows down the cooking of the zucchini. Use young tender zucchini.

INGREDIENTS

Serves 4
2 tablespoons corn oil
1 pound young zucchini, sliced
1 onion, finely chopped
2 garlic cloves, chopped
1 pound tomatoes, peeled, seeded and chopped
2 drained canned *jalapeño* peppers, rinsed, seeded and chopped
1 tablespoon chopped fresh cilantro
salt
fresh cilantro, to garnish

1 Heat the oil in a flameproof casserole and add all the remaining ingredients, except the salt.

2 Bring to simmering point, cover and cook over low heat for about 30 minutes until the zucchini are tender, checking from time to time that the dish is not drying out. If it is, add a little tomato juice, stock or water.

3 Season with salt and serve the Mexican way as a separate course. Alternatively, serve accompanied by any plainly cooked meat or poultry. Garnish with cilantro.

Refried Beans (Frijoles Refritos)

There is much disagreement about the translation of the term *refrito*. It means, literally, twice fried. Some cooks say this implies that the beans must be really well fried, others that it means twice cooked. However named, *Frijoles Refritos* are delicious.

INGREDIENTS

Serves 6–8
6–8 tablespoons lard or corn oil
1 onion, finely chopped
1 recipe Frijoles (cooked beans)

To garnish
freshly grated Parmesan cheese or crumbled farmer cheese
crisp-fried corn tortillas, cut into quarters

1 Heat 2 tablespoons of the lard in a large heavy frying pan and sauté the onion until it is soft and starting to turn translucent. Add about 1 cup of the Frijoles (cooked beans).

— COOK'S TIP —

Lard is the traditional (and best-tasting) fat for the beans, but many people prefer to use corn oil. Avoid using olive oil, which is too strongly flavored and distinctive.

2 Mash the beans with the back of a wooden spoon or potato masher, adding more beans and melted lard or oil until all the ingredients are used up and the beans have formed a heavy paste. Use extra lard if necessary.

3 Transfer to a warmed platter, piling the mixture up in a roll. Garnish with the cheese. Spike with the tortilla triangles, placing them at intervals along the length of the roll. Serve as a side dish.

Spicy Carrots

Adding spices to the carrots before leaving them to cool infuses them with flavor – an ideal dish to serve cold the next day (or up to a week later, if you keep it in the fridge).

INGREDIENTS

Serves 4

1 pound carrots
2 cups water
½ teaspoon salt
1 teaspoon cumin seeds
½–1 red chili (to taste)
1 large garlic clove, crushed
2 tablespoons olive oil
1 teaspoon paprika
juice of 1 lemon
flat leaf parsley, to garnish

1 Cut the carrots into slices about ¼-inch thick. Bring the water to a boil and add the salt and carrot slices. Simmer for about 8 minutes or until the carrots are just tender, without allowing them to get too soft. Drain the carrots, put them into a bowl and set aside until needed.

2 Grind or crush the cumin to a power. Remove the seeds from the chili and chop the chili finely. Take care when handling, as chilis can irritate the skin and eyes.

3 Gently heat the oil in a pan and toss in the garlic and the chili. Stir over medium heat for about a minute, without allowing the garlic to brown. Stir in the paprika and the lemon juice.

4 Pour the warm mixture over the carrots, tossing them well so they are coated with the spices. Spoon into a serving dish and garnish with a sprig of flat leaf parsley.

Kenyan Mung Bean Stew

The Kenyan name for this simple and tasty stew is *Dengu*.

INGREDIENTS

Serves 4

1¼ cups mung beans, soaked
   overnight
2 tablespoons ghee or butter
2 garlic cloves, crushed
1 red onion, chopped
2 tablespoons tomato paste
½ green bell pepper, seeded and cut
   into small cubes
½ red bell pepper, seeded and cut into
   small cubes
1 green chili, seeded and finely chopped

1 Put the mung beans in a large
saucepan, cover with water and
boil until the beans are very soft and
the water has evaporated. Remove
from the heat and mash with a fork or
potato masher until smooth.

2 Heat the ghee or butter in a
separate saucepan, add the garlic
and onion and fry for 4–5 minutes
until golden brown, then add the
tomato paste and cook for another
2–3 minutes, stirring constantly.

3 Stir in the mashed beans, then the
green and red peppers and chili.

4 Add 1¼ cups water, stirring well to
mix all the ingredients together.

5 Pour back into a clean saucepan
and simmer for about 10 minutes,
then spoon into a serving dish and
serve at once.

COOK'S TIP

Mung beans can be found in most Asian
stores. If unavailable, use whole green
lentils instead.

Fava Beans in Hot Sauce

A tasty dish of lima beans with a tomato and chili sauce.

INGREDIENTS

Serves 4

1 pound lima or fava beans, thawed
   if frozen
2 tablespoons olive oil
1 onion, finely chopped
2 garlic cloves, chopped
12 ounces tomatoes, peeled, seeded
   and chopped
1 or 2 drained canned *jalapeño* peppers,
   seeded and chopped
salt
chopped fresh cilantro sprigs,
   to garnish

1 Cook the beans in a saucepan of boiling water for 15–20 minutes, until tender. Drain and keep hot, to one side, in the covered saucepan.

2 Heat the olive oil in a frying pan and sauté the onion and garlic until the onion is soft but not brown. Add the tomatoes and cook until the mixture is thick and flavorful.

3 Add the *jalapeños* and cook for 1–2 minutes. Season with salt.

4 Pour the mixture over the reserved beans and check that they are hot. If not, return everything to the frying pan and cook over low heat just long enough to heat through. Put into a warm serving dish, garnish with cilantro and serve.

Fava Bean and Cauliflower Curry

This is a hot and spicy vegetable curry, ideal when served with cooked rice (especially a brown basmati variety), small poppadums and maybe a cooling cucumber raita as well.

INGREDIENTS

Serves 4

2 garlic cloves, chopped
1-inch cube fresh ginger
1 fresh green chili, seeded and chopped
1 tablespoon oil
1 onion, sliced
1 large potato, chopped
2 tablespoons ghee or softened butter
1 tablespoon curry powder, mild or hot
1 cauliflower, cut into small florets
2½ cups stock
2 tablespoons creamed coconut
10-ounce can fava beans, with liquor
juice of ½ lemon (optional)
salt and ground black pepper
fresh cilantro or parsley, chopped,
    to garnish

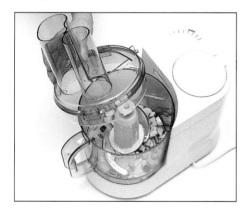

1 Blend the garlic, ginger, chili and oil in a food processor or blender until they form a smooth paste.

2 In a large saucepan, fry the onion and potato in the ghee or butter for 5 minutes, then stir in the spice paste and curry powder. Cook for 1 minute.

3 Add the cauliflower florets and stir well into the spicy mixture, then pour in the stock. Bring to a boil and mix in the creamed coconut, stirring until it melts.

4 Season well, then cover and simmer for 10 minutes. Add the beans and their liquor and cook, uncovered, for 10 minutes more.

5 Check the seasoning and add a good squeeze of lemon juice, if liked. Serve hot, garnished with cilantro or parsley.

Masala Mashed Potatoes

These potatoes are very versatile and will perk up any meal.

INGREDIENTS

Serves 4

3 potatoes
1 tablespoon chopped fresh mint
   and cilantro, mixed
1 teaspoon mango powder
1 teaspoon salt
1 teaspoon crushed black peppercorns
1 fresh red chili, chopped
1 fresh green chili, chopped
4 tablespoons margarine

1 Boil the potatoes until soft enough to be mashed. Mash them down using a masher.

2 Blend together the chopped herbs, mango powder, salt, pepper, chilies and margarine to form a paste.

3 Stir the mixture into the mashed potatoes and mix together thoroughly with a fork. Serve warm as an accompaniment.

VARIATION

Instead of potatoes, try sweet potatoes. Cook them until tender, mash and continue from step 2.

Spicy Cabbage

An excellent vegetable accompaniment, this is a very versatile spicy dish that can also be served as a warm side salad. It's so quick to make that it can be a handy last minute addition to any meal.

INGREDIENTS

Serves 4

4 tablespoons margarine
½ teaspoon white cumin seeds
3–8 dried red chilies, to taste
1 small onion, sliced
2½ cups cabbage, shredded
2 carrots, grated
½ teaspoon salt
2 tablespoons lemon juice

1 Melt the margarine in a saucepan and fry the white cumin seeds and dried red chilies for about 30 seconds.

2 Add the sliced onion and fry for about 2 minutes. Add the cabbage and carrots and stir-fry for 5 minutes more until the cabbage is soft.

3 Finally, stir in the salt and lemon juice, and serve.

Vinegared Chili Cabbage

A hot cabbage dish that adds a bit of spice to every meal. The addition of vinegar at the end gives this dish its distinct flavour.

INGREDIENTS

Serves 4–6
1 fresh red chili, halved, seeded and shredded
2 tablespoons vegetable shortening or butter
2 garlic cloves, crushed (optional)
1 white cabbage, cored and shredded
2 teaspoons cider vinegar
1 teaspoon cayenne pepper
salt

COOK'S TIP

A wok with a domed lid is good for this part-frying, part-steaming method of cooking cabbage.

1 Put the chili with the shortening or butter into a large pan and cook over medium heat until the chili sizzles and curls at the edges.

2 Add the garlic and cabbage and stir, over the heat, until the cabbage is coated and warm. Add salt to taste and 5 tablespoons water. Bring to a boil, cover and lower the heat.

3 Cook, shaking the pan regularly, for 3–4 minutes until the cabbage wilts. Remove the lid, raise the heat and cook off the liquid. Check the seasoning and sprinkle with vinegar and cayenne pepper.

Coleslaw in Triple-hot Dressing

The triple hotness in this coleslaw is supplied by mustard, horseradish and Tabasco.

INGREDIENTS

Serves 6
½ white cabbage, cored and shredded
2 celery stalks, finely sliced
1 green bell pepper, seeded and finely sliced
4 scallions, shredded
2 tablespoons chopped fresh dill
cayenne pepper

For the dressing
1 tablespoon Dijon mustard
2 teaspoons horseradish
1 teaspoon Tabasco sauce
2 tablespoons red wine vinegar
5 tablespoons olive oil
salt and ground black pepper

1 Mix the cabbage, celery, bell pepper and scallions in a bowl.

2 Mix the mustard, horseradish and Tabasco sauce, then gradually stir in the vinegar with a fork and finally beat in the oil and seasoning. Toss the salad in the dressing and let stand, if possible, for at least 1 hour, turning it once or twice.

3 Immediately before serving, season the salad if necessary, toss again and sprinkle with dill and cayenne.

COOK'S TIP

This is a good salad for a buffet table or picnic as it improves after standing in its dressing (it could be left overnight in the fridge) and travels well in a covered plastic bowl or box.

Vegetables in Peanut and Chili Sauce

INGREDIENTS

Serves 4

1 tablespoon palm or vegetable oil
1 onion, chopped
2 garlic cloves, crushed
14-ounce can tomatoes, puréed
3 tablespoons smooth peanut butter,
  preferably unsalted
3²/₃ cups water
1 teaspoon dried thyme
1 green chili, seeded and chopped
1 vegetable stock cube
¹/₂ teaspoon ground allspice
2 carrots
4 ounces white cabbage
6 ounces okra
¹/₂ red bell pepper, seeded
²/₃ cup vegetable stock
salt

1 Heat the oil in a large saucepan and fry the onion and garlic over a moderate heat for 5 minutes, stirring frequently. Add the tomatoes and peanut butter and stir well.

2 Stir in the water, thyme, chili, stock cube, allspice and a little salt. Bring to a boil and then simmer gently, uncovered, for about 35 minutes.

3 Cut the carrots into sticks, slice the cabbage, remove the ends of the okra, and seed and slice the red pepper.

4 Place the vegetables in a saucepan with the stock, bring to a boil and cook until they are just tender but still with a little "bite".

5 Drain the vegetables and place in a warmed serving dish. Pour the sauce over the top and serve.

Marinated Vegetables on Skewers

These kebabs are a delightful main dish for vegetarians, or can be served as a vegetable side dish.

INGREDIENTS

Serves 4
4 ounces pumpkin
1 red onion
1 small zucchini
1 ripe plantain
1 eggplant
½ red bell pepper, seeded
½ green bell pepper, seeded
12 button mushrooms
4 tablespoons lemon juice
4 tablespoons olive or sunflower oil
3–4 tablespoons soy sauce
⅔ cup tomato juice
1 green chili, seeded and chopped
½ onion, grated
3 garlic cloves, crushed
1½ teaspoons dried tarragon, crushed
¾ teaspoon dried basil
¾ teaspoon dried thyme
¾ teaspoon ground cinnamon
2 tablespoons butter or margarine
1¼ cups vegetable stock
freshly ground black pepper
fresh parsley sprigs, to garnish

1 Peel and cube the pumpkin, place in a small bowl and cover with boiling water. Blanch for 2–3 minutes, then drain and refresh under cold water.

2 Cut the onion into wedges, slice the zucchini and plantain and cut the eggplant and red and green peppers into chunks. Trim the mushrooms. Place the vegetables, including the pumpkin in a large bowl.

3 Mix together the lemon juice, oil, soy sauce, tomato juice, chili, grated onion, garlic, herbs, cinnamon and black pepper and pour over the vegetables. Toss together and then set aside in a cool place to marinate for a few hours.

4 Thread the vegetables on to eight skewers, using a variety of vegetables on each to make a colorful display. Preheat the broiler.

5 Broil the vegetables under a low heat, for about 15 minutes, turning frequently, until golden brown, basting with the marinade to keep the vegetables moist.

6 Place the remaining marinade, butter or margarine and stock in a pan and simmer for 10 minutes to cook the onion and reduce the sauce.

7 Pour the sauce into a serving pitcher and arrange the vegetable skewers on a plate. Garnish with parsley and serve with a rice dish or salad.

COOK'S TIP

You can use any vegetable that you prefer. Just first parboil any that may require longer cooking.

Black-eyed Pea Stew with Spicy Pumpkin

INGREDIENTS

Serves 3–4

1¼ cups black-eyed peas, soaked for 4
  hours or overnight
1 onion, chopped
1 green or red bell pepper, seeded and
  chopped
2 garlic cloves, chopped
1 vegetable stock cube
1 thyme sprig or 1 teaspoon dried thyme
1 teaspoon paprika
½ teaspoon allspice
2 carrots, sliced
1–2 tablespoons palm oil
salt and hot pepper sauce

For the spicy pumpkin

1½ pounds pumpkin
1 onion
2 tablespoons butter or margarine
2 garlic cloves, crushed
3 tomatoes, peeled and chopped
½ teaspoon ground cinnamon
2 teaspoons curry powder
pinch of grated nutmeg
⅔ cup water
salt, hot pepper sauce and freshly
  ground black pepper

1 Drain the peas, place in a pan and
cover generously with water. Bring
the peas to a boil.

2 Add the onion, green or red
pepper, garlic, stock cube, herbs
and spices. Simmer for 45 minutes or
until the peas are just tender. Season to
taste with the salt and a little hot
pepper sauce.

3 Add the carrots and palm oil and
continue cooking for about
10–12 minutes until the carrots are
cooked, adding a little more water if
necessary. Remove from the heat and
set aside.

4 To make the spicy pumpkin, cut
the pumpkin into cubes and finely
chop the onion.

5 Melt the butter or margarine in a
frying pan or saucepan, and add
the pumpkin, onion, garlic, tomatoes,
spices and water. Stir well to combine
and simmer until the pumpkin is soft.
Season with salt, hot pepper sauce and
black pepper, to taste. Serve with the
black-eyed peas.

Red Bean Chili

This vegetarian chili can be adapted to accommodate meat eaters by adding either ground beef or lamb in place of the lentils. Add the meat once the onions are soft and fry until well-browned before adding the tomatoes.

INGREDIENTS

Serves 4

2 tablespoons vegetable oil
1 onion, chopped
14-ounce can chopped tomatoes
2 garlic cloves, crushed
1¼ cups white wine
1¼ cups vegetable stock
4 ounces red lentils
2 thyme sprigs or 1 teaspoon dried
   thyme
2 teaspoons ground cumin
3 tablespoons dark soy sauce
½ hot chili pepper, finely chopped
1 teaspoon five-spice powder
1 tablespoon oyster sauce (optional)
8-ounce can red kidney beans, drained
2 teaspoons sugar
salt

1 Heat the oil in a large saucepan and fry the onion over a moderate heat for a few minutes until slightly softened.

2 Add the tomatoes and garlic, cook for 10 minutes, then stir in the wine and stock.

3 Add the lentils, thyme, cumin, soy sauce, hot pepper, five-spice powder and oyster sauce, if using.

4 Cover and simmer for 40 minutes or until the lentils are cooked, stirring occasionally and adding more water if the lentils begin to dry out.

5 Stir in the kidney beans and sugar and continue cooking for about 10 minutes, adding extra stock or water if necessary. Season to taste with salt and serve hot with boiled rice.

COOK'S TIP

Fiery chilies can irritate the skin, so always wash your hands well after handling them and take care not to touch your eyes. If you like really hot, spicy food, then add the seeds from the chili, too.

Chiles Rellenos

INGREDIENTS

Serves 4

8 large green bell peppers or fresh green chilies such as poblano
1–2 tablespoons vegetable oil, plus extra for frying
4 cups grated cheese
4 eggs, separated
²/₃ cup flour

For the sauce

1 tablespoon vegetable oil
1 small onion, chopped
¼ teaspoon salt
1–2 teaspoons red pepper flakes
½ teaspoon ground cumin
1 cup beef or chicken stock
3 cups canned peeled tomatoes

COOK'S TIP

If necessary, work in batches, but do not coat the peppers until you are ready to fry them.

1 For the sauce, heat the oil in a frying pan. Add the onion and cook over low heat for 8 minutes until just soft. Stir in the salt, pepper flakes, cumin, stock and tomatoes. Cover and simmer gently for about 5 minutes, stirring occasionally.

2 Transfer the mixture to a food processor or blender and process until smooth. Strain into a clean saucepan. Taste for seasoning, and set aside. Preheat the broiler.

3 Brush the peppers or chilies with oil. Lay them on a baking sheet. Broil as close to the heat as possible for 5–8 minutes until blackened all over. Cover with a dish towel and set aside.

4 When cool enough to handle, remove the charred skin. Carefully slit the bell peppers or chilies and scoop out the seeds.

5 With your hands, form the cheese into eight cylinders that are slightly shorter than the peppers. Place the cheese cylinders inside the peppers. Secure the slits with toothpicks. Set aside.

6 Beat the egg whites until just stiff. Add the egg yolks, one at a time, beating on low speed to incorporate them. Beat in 1 tablespoon flour.

7 Put a 1-inch layer of oil in a frying pan. Heat until hot but not smoking (to test, drop a little batter in the oil: if the oil sizzles, it is hot enough for frying).

8 Coat the peppers lightly in flour all over, shaking off any excess. Dip into the egg batter, then place in the hot oil. Fry for about 2 minutes until brown on one side. Turn carefully and brown the other side.

9 Reheat the sauce and serve with the *Chiles Rellenos*.

VARIATION

If using bell peppers instead of green chilies, mix the grated cheese with 1 tablespoon hot chili powder for a more authentic Southwest taste.

Stir-fried Chili Greens

This attractive dish is spiced with ginger and red chilies, and given added zest by the addition of oyster sauce.

INGREDIENTS

Serves 4

2 bunches spinach or chard or 1 head Chinese cabbage
3 garlic cloves, crushed
2 inches fresh ginger root, peeled and cut in matchsticks
3–4 tablespoons peanut oil
14 ounces boneless, skinless chicken breast, or pork loin, or a mixture of both, very finely sliced
12 quail's eggs, hard-boiled and shelled
1 fresh red chili, seeded and shredded
2–3 tablespoons oyster sauce
1 tablespoon brown sugar
2 teaspoons cornstarch, mixed with ¼ cup cold water
salt

— COOK'S TIP —

As with all stir-fries, don't start cooking until you have prepared all the ingredients and arranged them to hand. Cut everything into small, even-size pieces so the food can be cooked very quickly and all the colors and flavors preserved.

1 Wash the chosen leaves well and shake them dry. Strip the tender leaves from the stems and tear them into pieces. Discard the lower, tougher part of the stems and slice the remainder evenly.

2 Fry the garlic and ginger in the hot oil, without browning, for a minute. Add the chicken and/or pork and keep stirring it in the wok until the meat changes color. When the meat looks cooked, add the sliced stems first and cook them quickly; then add the torn leaves, quail's eggs and chili. Spoon in the oyster sauce and a little boiling water, if necessary. Cover and cook for 1–2 minutes only.

3 Remove the lid, stir and add sugar and salt to taste. Stir in the cornstarch and water mixture and toss thoroughly. Cook until the mixture is well coated in a glossy sauce.

4 Serve immediately, while still very hot and the colors are bright and glowingly jewel-like.

Green Bean and Chili Pepper Salad

INGREDIENTS

Serves 4

12 ounces cooked green beans,
    quartered
2 red peppers, seeded and chopped
2 scallions (white and green parts),
    chopped
1 or more drained pickled *serrano*
    chilies, well rinsed, seeded and
    chopped
1 iceberg lettuce, coarsely shredded, or
    mixed salad leaves
olives, to garnish

For the dressing

3 tablespoons red wine vinegar
9 tablespoons olive oil
salt and freshly ground black pepper

1 Combine the cooked green beans,
chopped peppers, chopped
scallions and chilies in a salad bowl.

2 Make the salad dressing. Pour the
red wine vinegar into a bowl or
cup. Add salt and freshly ground black
pepper to taste, then gradually whisk in
the olive oil until well combined.

3 Pour the salad dressing over the
prepared vegetables and toss lightly
together to mix and coat thoroughly.

4 Line a large platter with the
shredded lettuce leaves and arrange
the salad attractively on top. Garnish
with the olives and serve.

Mushrooms with Chipotle Chilies

INGREDIENTS

Serves 6

4 cups button mushrooms
4 tablespoons olive oil
1 onion, finely chopped
2 garlic cloves, chopped
2 drained canned *chipotle* chilies, rinsed
   and sliced
salt
chopped fresh cilantro, to garnish

> ───── COOK'S TIP ─────
>
> Never wash mushrooms, as they quickly
> absorb water. Wipe them with a paper
> towel or a clean, damp cloth.

1 Wipe the mushrooms gently and carefully with kitchen paper. Heat the olive oil in a large heavy frying pan and add the mushrooms, onion, garlic, and sliced *chipotles*. Stir to coat the vegetables in oil.

2 Fry the mixture over medium heat for 6–8 minutes, stirring from time to time, until the onions and mushrooms are tender. Season to taste with salt and serve on small individual plates, sprinkled with a little chopped fresh cilantro.

Jalapeño and Shrimp Salad

Pickled jalapeño chili gives a distinctive spicy flavor to this delicious salad. In Mexico, it is quite usual to serve such a hearty salad as a separate course.

INGREDIENTS

Serves 4

1 iceberg lettuce, separated into leaves,
   or assorted lettuce leaves
¼ cup mayonnaise
¼ cup sour cream
12 ounces cooked shrimp,
   chopped
½ cup chopped cooked green beans
½ cup chopped cooked carrots
½ cucumber, about 4 ounces
   chopped
2 hard-cooked eggs, coarsely
   chopped
1 drained pickled *jalapeño* pepper,
   seeded and chopped
salt

1 Line a large salad bowl or platter with the lettuce leaves. Stir together the mayonnaise and sour cream in a small bowl and set aside.

2 Combine the shrimp, beans, carrot, cucumber, eggs and *jalapeño* in a separate bowl. Season with salt.

3 Add the mayonnaise and sour cream mixture to the shrimp, folding it in very gently so that all the ingredients are well mixed and coated with the dressing. Pile the mixture into the lined salad bowl or arrange attractively on the platter and serve.

Spicy Potato Salad

This tasty salad is quick to prepare, and makes a satisfying accompaniment to grilled or barbecued meat or fish.

INGREDIENTS

Serves 6

2 pounds potatoes, peeled
2 red bell peppers
2 celery stalks
1 shallot
2 or 3 scallions
1 green chili, finely chopped
1 garlic clove, crushed
2 teaspoons finely chopped
   fresh chives
2 teaspoons finely chopped
   fresh basil
1 tablespoon finely chopped fresh
   parsley
1 tablespoon light cream
3 tablespoons mayonnaise
1 teaspoon mild mustard
½ tablespoon sugar
chopped fresh chives, to garnish

1 Boil the potatoes until tender but still firm. Drain and cool, then cut into 1-inch cubes and place in a large salad bowl.

2 Halve the peppers, cut away and discard the core and seeds and cut into small pieces. Finely chop the celery, shallot, and scallions and slice the chili very thinly, discarding the seeds. Add the vegetables to the cubed potatoes together with the garlic and chopped herbs.

3 Blend together the cream, mayonnaise, mustard and sugar in a small bowl, stirring until the mixture is well combined.

4 Pour the dressing over the potato and vegetable salad and stir gently to coat evenly. Serve, garnished with the chopped chives.

Peppery Bean Salad

This pretty salad uses canned beans for speed and convenience.

INGREDIENTS

Serves 4–6

15-ounce can kidney beans, drained
15-ounce can black-eyed peas, drained
15-ounce can chick-peas, drained
¼ red bell pepper
¼ green bell pepper
6 radishes
1 tablespoon chopped scallion
1 teaspoon ground cumin
1 tablespoon tomato ketchup
2 tablespoons olive oil
1 tablespoon white wine vinegar
1 garlic clove, crushed
½ teaspoon hot pepper sauce
salt
sliced scallion, to garnish

1 Drain the canned beans and chick-peas and rinse under cold running water. Shake off the excess water and turn them into a large salad bowl.

2 Core, seed and chop the peppers. Trim the radishes and slice thinly. Add to the beans with the pepper and scallion.

3 Mix together the cumin, ketchup, oil, vinegar and garlic in a small bowl. Add a little salt and hot pepper sauce to taste and stir again thoroughly.

4 Pour the dressing over the salad and mix. Chill for at least 1 hour before serving, garnished with scallion.

--- COOK'S TIP ---

For an even tastier salad, allow the ingredients to marinate for a few hours.

Balti Potatoes

Balti is a traditional way of cooking Indian curries in a karahi cooking pan.

INGREDIENTS

Serves 4

3 tablespoons corn oil
½ teaspoon white cumin seeds
3 curry leaves
1 teaspoon crushed dried red chilies
½ teaspoon mixed onion, mustard and fenugreek seeds
½ teaspoon fennel seeds
3 garlic cloves
½ teaspoon shredded ginger
2 onions, sliced
6 new potatoes, sliced thinly
1 tablespoon chopped fresh cilantro
1 fresh red chili, seeded and sliced
1 fresh green chili, seeded and sliced

1 Heat the oil in a deep round-bottomed frying pan or a karahi. Lower the heat slightly and add the cumin seeds, curry leaves, dried red chilies, mixed onion, mustard and fenugreek seeds, fennel seeds, garlic cloves and ginger. Fry for 1 minute, then add the onions and fry for 5 minutes more, or until the onions are golden brown.

2 Add the potatoes, fresh cilantro and fresh red and green chilies and mix well. Cover the pan tightly with a lid or foil, making sure the foil does not touch the food. Cook over very low heat for about 7 minutes, or until the potatoes are tender.

3 Remove the pan from the heat, take off the foil and serve hot.

Okra with Green Mango and Lentils

If you like okra, you'll love this spicy tangy dish. Serve it with Indian meat or fish dishes, vegetables, breads and rice.

INGREDIENTS

Serves 4

½ cup yellow lentils (toor dhal)
3 tablespoons corn oil
½ teaspoon onion seeds
2 onions, sliced
½ teaspoon ground fenugreek
1 teaspoon ginger pulp
1 teaspoon garlic pulp
1½ teaspoons chili powder
¼ teaspoon turmeric
1 teaspoon ground coriander
1 green mango, peeled and sliced
1 pound okra, cut into ½-inch pieces
1½ teaspoons salt
2 fresh red chilies, seeded and sliced
2 tablespoons chopped fresh cilantro
1 tomato, sliced

1 Wash the lentils thoroughly and put in a saucepan with enough water to cover. Bring to a boil and cook until soft but not mushy. Drain and set to one side.

2 Heat the oil in a deep round-bottomed frying pan or a karahi and fry the onion seeds until they begin to pop. Add the onions and fry until golden brown. Lower the heat and add the ground fenugreek, ginger, garlic, chili powder, turmeric and ground coriander.

3 Throw in the mango slices and the okra. Stir well and add the salt, red chilies and fresh cilantro. Stir-fry for about 3 minutes, or until the okra is well cooked.

4 Finally, add the cooked lentils and sliced tomato and cook for 3 minutes more. Serve hot.

Spicy Vegetables with Almonds

INGREDIENTS

Serves 4

2 tablespoons vegetable oil
2 onions, sliced
2-inch piece of fresh ginger, shredded
1 teaspoon crushed black peppercorns
1 bay leaf
¼ teaspoon turmeric
1 teaspoon ground coriander
1 teaspoon salt
½ teaspoon garam masala
2½ cups mushrooms, sliced
1 zucchini, thickly sliced
2 ounces green beans, sliced into
   1-inch pieces
1 tablespoon chopped fresh mint
⅔ cup water
2 tablespoons plain low-fat yogurt
¼ cup slivered almonds

1 In a medium deep frying pan, heat the vegetable oil and add the sliced onions with the shredded fresh ginger, crushed black peppercorns and the bay leaf. Gently fry for 3–5 minutes, stirring constantly.

2 Lower the heat and add the turmeric, ground coriander, salt and garam masala, stirring occasionally. Gradually add the mushrooms, zucchini, green beans and the mint. Stir gently so that the vegetables retain their shape.

3 Pour in the water and bring to a simmer, then lower the heat and cook until most of the water has evaporated.

4 Beat the plain low-fat yogurt well with a fork, then pour it onto the vegetables in the saucepan and mix together well.

5 Cook the spicy vegetables for 2–3 minutes more, stirring occasionally. Sprinkle with slivered almonds and serve.

—————— COOK'S TIP ——————

For an extra creamy dish, add sour cream instead of the plain yogurt.

Masala Beans with Fenugreek

"Masala" means spice and this vegetarian dish is spicy, though not necessarily hot. You can adapt the spiciness of the dish by using smaller or larger quantities of the spices, as you wish. Serve it as an accompaniment to a meat dish with freshly cooked basmati rice for a wonderful Indian meal.

INGREDIENTS

Serves 4

1 onion
1 teaspoon ground cumin
1 teaspoon ground coriander
1 teaspoon sesame seeds
1 teaspoon chili powder
½ teaspoon garlic pulp
¼ teaspoon turmeric
1 teaspoon salt
2 tablespoons vegetable oil
1 tomato, quartered
8 ounces green beans
1 bunch fresh fenugreek leaves,
　stems discarded
4 tablespoons chopped fresh cilantro
1 tablespoon lemon juice

1 Coarsely chop the onion. In a mixing bowl, combine the ground cumin and coriander, sesame seeds, chili powder, garlic pulp, turmeric and salt. Mix well.

2 Place all of these ingredients, including the onion, in a food processor or blender and process for 30–45 seconds.

3 In a medium saucepan, heat the vegetable oil and fry the spice mixture for about 5 minutes, stirring it occasionally as it cooks.

4 Add the quartered tomato, green beans, fresh fenugreek and fresh chopped cilantro.

5 Stir-fry the mixture for about 5 minutes, then sprinkle over the lemon juice, pour into a serving dish and serve immediately.

------ COOK'S TIP ------

If you can't find fenugreek leaves, use 1 teaspoon fenugreek seeds instead.

FLAME-FILLED RICE AND NOODLES

Rice and noodles are the cornerstones of many cuisines and their unassertive taste lends itself to flavoring with mild or hot spices, or a mixture of both. Many of the classic rice dishes appear: Nasi Goreng, Chicken Jambalaya and Sushi, seasoned with the breathtaking wasabi paste. Noodle dishes are justly popular in Thailand and China where they are combined with chilies, limes, sesame oil, cilantro and many other emphatic ingredients to produce such delights as Spicy Szechuan Noodles and Thai Fried Noodles.

Yogurt Chicken and Rice

This is flavored with *zereshk*, small dried berries available at Middle Eastern stores.

INGREDIENTS

Serves 6
3 tablespoons butter
3–3½ pounds chicken pieces
1 large onion, chopped
1 cup chicken stock
2 eggs
2 cups plain yogurt
2–3 saffron strands, dissolved in
   1 tablespoon boiling water
1 teaspoon ground cinnamon
generous 2¼ cups basmati rice,
   soaked in salted water for 2 hours
3 ounces *zereshk*
salt and freshly ground black pepper
herb salad, to serve

1 Melt two-thirds of the butter in a casserole and fry the chicken and onion for 4–5 minutes, until the onion is softened and the chicken browned.

2 Add the stock and salt and pepper, bring to a boil and then simmer for 45 minutes, or until the chicken is cooked and the stock reduced by half.

3 Skin and bone the chicken. Cut the flesh into large pieces and place in a large bowl. Reserve the stock.

4 Beat the eggs and blend with the yogurt. Add the saffron water and cinnamon and season with salt and pepper. Pour over the chicken and leave to marinate on one side for up to 2 hours.

5 Drain the rice and then boil in salted water for 5 minutes, reduce the heat and simmer very gently for 10 minutes, until half cooked. Drain and rinse in warm water.

6 Transfer the chicken from the yogurt mixture to a dish and mix half the rice into the yogurt.

7 Preheat the oven to 325°F and grease a large 4-inch-deep casserole.

8 Place the rice and yogurt mixture in the bottom of the dish, arrange the chicken pieces on top and then add the plain rice. Warm the *zereshk* and sprinkle over the top.

9 Mix the remaining butter with the chicken stock and pour over the rice. Cover tightly with foil and cook in the oven for 35–45 minutes.

10 Leave the dish to cool for a few minutes. Place on a cold, damp dish towel, which will help lift the rice from the base of the dish, then run a knife around the inside edge of the dish. Place a large flat plate over the dish and turn out. You should have a rice "cake," which can be cut into wedges. Serve hot with an herb salad.

Louisiana Rice

Eggplant and pork are featured in this highly-seasoned dish.

INGREDIENTS

Serves 4

4 tablespoons vegetable oil
1 small eggplant, diced
8 ounces ground pork
1 green bell pepper, seeded and
　chopped
2 ribs celery, chopped
1 onion, chopped
1 garlic clove, crushed
1 teaspoon cayenne pepper
1 teaspoon paprika
1 teaspoon freshly ground black pepper
½ teaspoon salt
1 teaspoon dried thyme
½ teaspoon dried oregano
2 cups chicken stock
8 ounces chicken livers, minced
scant ⅔ cup long-grain rice
1 bay leaf
3 tablespoons chopped fresh parsley
celery leaves, to garnish

1 Heat the oil in a frying pan until piping hot, then add the eggplant and stir-fry for about 5 minutes.

2 Add the pork and cook for 6–8 minutes until browned, using a wooden spoon to break up any lumps.

3 Add the green pepper, celery, onion, garlic and all the spices and herbs. Cover and cook over high heat for 5–6 minutes, stirring frequently from the base of the pan to scrape up and distribute the crispy brown bits.

4 Pour in the chicken stock and stir to remove any sediment from the base of the pan. Cover and cook for 6 minutes over a moderate heat. Stir in the chicken livers, cook for 2 minutes, then stir in the rice and add the bay leaf.

5 Reduce the heat, cover and simmer for 6–7 minutes. Turn off the heat and let stand for another 10–15 minutes, until the rice is tender. Remove the bay leaf and stir in the chopped parsley. Serve the rice hot, garnished with the celery leaves.

Spicy Fish and Rice

This Arabic fish dish, *Sayadich,* is especially popular in Lebanon.

INGREDIENTS

Serves 4–6
juice of 1 lemon
3 tablespoons olive oil
2 pounds cod steaks
4 large onions, chopped
1 teaspoon ground cumin
2–3 saffron strands
4 cups fish stock
generous 2¼ cups basmati or other
    long-grain rice
¼ cup pine nuts, lightly toasted
salt and freshly ground black pepper
fresh parsley, to garnish

1 Blend the lemon juice and 1 tablespoon of the oil in a shallow dish. Add the fish, turning to coat thoroughly. Cover and marinate for 30 minutes.

2 Heat the remaining oil in a large saucepan and fry the onions for 5–6 minutes, stirring occasionally.

3 Drain the fish, reserving the marinade, and add to the pan. Fry for 1–2 minutes per side until lightly golden, then add the cumin, saffron strands and a little salt and pepper.

4 Pour in the fish stock and the reserved marinade, bring to a boil and then simmer for 5–10 minutes or until the fish is nearly done.

5 Transfer the fish to a plate and add the rice to the stock. Bring to a boil, reduce the heat and simmer gently for 15 minutes until nearly all the stock has been absorbed.

6 Arrange the fish on top of the rice and cover the pan. Steam over low heat for 15–20 minutes.

7 Transfer the fish to a plate, then spoon the rice onto a large flat dish and arrange the fish on top. Sprinkle with toasted pine nuts and garnish with fresh parsley.

Masala Shrimp and Rice

INGREDIENTS

Serves 4–6
2 large onions, sliced and deep-fried
1¼ cups plain yogurt
2 tablespoons tomato paste
4 tablespoons green masala paste
2 tablespoons lemon juice
1 teaspoon black cumin seeds
2-inch cinnamon stick
4 green cardamom pods
1 pound fresh jumbo shrimp, peeled
    and deveined
3 cups button mushrooms
2 cups frozen peas, thawed
generous 2¼ cups basmati rice soaked
    for 5 minutes in boiled water and
    drained
1¼ cups water
1 sachet saffron powder mixed in
    6 tablespoons milk
2 tablespoon ghee or unsalted butter
salt, to taste

1 Combine the first 9 ingredients together in a large bowl. Stir the shrimp, mushrooms and peas into the marinade and leave for about 2 hours.

2 Grease the base of a heavy pan and add the shrimp, vegetables and any marinade juices. Cover with the drained rice and smooth the surface gently until you have an even layer.

3 Pour the water all over the surface of the rice. Make random holes through the rice with the handle of a spoon and pour in the saffron milk.

4 Place a few knobs of ghee or butter on the surface and place a circular piece of foil directly on top of the rice. Cover and steam over a low heat for 45–50 minutes, until the rice is cooked Gently toss the rice, shrimp and vegetables together and serve hot.

Spiced Trout Pilaf

Smoked trout might seem to be an unusual partner for rice, but this is a winning combination.

INGREDIENTS

Serves 4

generous 1 cup basmati rice
3 tablespoons butter
2 onions, sliced into rings
1 garlic clove, crushed
2 bay leaves
2 whole cloves
2 green cardamom pods
2-inch cinnamon stick
1 teaspoon cumin seeds
4 smoked trout fillets, skinned
$\frac{1}{2}$ cup slivered almonds, toasted
scant $\frac{1}{2}$ cup seedless raisins
2 tablespoons chopped
   fresh parsley
mango chutney, to serve
poppadums, to serve

1 Wash the rice thoroughly in several changes of water and drain well. Set aside. Melt the butter in a large frying pan and fry the onions until well browned, stirring frequently.

2 Add the garlic, bay leaves, cloves, cardamom pods, cinnamon and cumin seeds and stir-fry for 1 minute.

3 Stir in the rice, then add 2½ cups boiling water. Bring to a boil. Cover the pan tightly, reduce the heat and cook very gently for 20–25 minutes, until the water has been absorbed and the rice is tender.

4 Flake the trout and add to the pan with the almonds and raisins. Fluff the rice with a fork to distribute. Cover the pan and allow the smoked trout to warm in the rice for a few minutes. Sprinkle with the parsley and serve with mango chutney and poppadums.

Nasi Goreng

One of the most popular and well-known Indonesian dishes, nasi goreng is a great way to use up leftover rice, chicken and meats such as pork.

INGREDIENTS

Serves 4–6

scant 1½ cups (dry-weight) basmati rice, cooked and cooled
2 eggs
2 tablespoons water
7 tablespoons vegetable oil
8 ounces pork or beef fillet
2–3 fresh red chili peppers, seeded and sliced
½-inch cube terasi (shrimp paste)
2 garlic cloves, crushed
1 onion, sliced
1 cup cooked, peeled shrimp
1½ cups chopped cooked chicken
2 tablespoons dark soy sauce or 3–4 tablespoons tomato ketchup
salt and freshly ground black pepper
celery leaves, deep-fried onions and fresh cilantro sprigs, to garnish

1 Separate the grains of the cooked and cooled rice with a fork. Cover and set aside until needed.

2 Beat the eggs with the water and season lightly with salt and pepper. With a minimum of oil, make two or three thin omelettes in a frying pan. Let cool. When cold, roll up each omelette and cut into strips. Set aside.

3 Cut the pork or beef fillet into neat strips. Finely shred one of the sliced chilies and set aside.

4 Put the terasi, with the remaining chili, the garlic and onion, in a food processor, or use a mortar and pestle, and grind to a fine paste.

5 Heat the remaining oil in a wok and fry the paste, without browning, until it gives off a rich, spicy aroma. Add the pork or beef, tossing the meat constantly, to seal in the juices. Cook for 2 minutes, stirring constantly. Add the shrimp, cook for 2 minutes and then stir in the chicken, cold rice, dark soy sauce or ketchup and season to taste. Stir constantly to keep the rice light and fluffy and prevent it from sticking.

6 Turn onto a hot serving plate and garnish with the omelette strips, celery leaves, onions, reserved shredded chili and the cilantro sprigs.

Seafood and Rice

INGREDIENTS

Serves 4

2 tablespoons olive oil
4 ounces bacon, rind removed, diced
1 onion, chopped
2 stalks celery, chopped
2 large garlic cloves, chopped
1 teaspoon cayenne pepper
2 bay leaves
1 teaspoon dried oregano
½ teaspoon dried thyme
4 tomatoes, peeled and chopped
⅔ cup tomato sauce
scant 1 cup long-grain rice
2 cups fish stock
6 ounces cod or haddock, skinned,
   boned and cubed
1 cup cooked peeled shrimp
salt and freshly ground black pepper
2 green onions, chopped,
   to garnish

1 Preheat the oven to 350°F. Heat the oil in a large saucepan and fry the bacon until crisp. Add the onion and celery and stir until the vegetables begin to stick to the pan.

2 Add the garlic, cayenne pepper, herbs, tomatoes and seasoning and mix well. Stir in the tomato sauce, rice and broth and bring to the boil.

3 Gently stir in the fish and transfer to an ovenproof dish. Cover tightly with foil and bake for 20–30 minutes, until the rice is just tender. Stir in the shrimp and heat through. Serve topped with the green onions.

Chicken Jambalaya

INGREDIENTS

Serves 10

2 chickens (3½ pounds each)
1 pound raw smoked ham
4 tablespoons lard or bacon fat
½ cup all-purpose flour
3 onions, finely sliced
2 green bell peppers, seeded and sliced
1½ pounds tomatoes, chopped
2–3 garlic cloves, crushed
2 teaspoons chopped fresh thyme or
   1 teaspoon dried thyme
24 medium shrimp, peeled
scant 3 cups long-grain rice
4½ cups cold water
2–3 dashes Tabasco sauce
6 green onions, finely chopped
3 tablespoons chopped fresh parsley
salt and freshly ground black pepper

1 Cut each chicken into 10 pieces and season with salt and pepper. Dice the ham; discard the rind and fat.

2 In a large casserole over medium-high heat, melt the lard and brown the chicken pieces all over, setting them aside as they are done.

3 Reduce the heat, sprinkle the flour over the fat in the pan and stir until the roux is deep golden brown.

4 Return the chicken pieces to the pan, add the diced ham, onions, green peppers, tomatoes, garlic and thyme and cook, stirring regularly, for 10 minutes, then stir in the shrimp.

5 Add the rice to the pan along with the water and stir to combine. Season with salt, pepper and Tabasco sauce. Bring to a boil and cook over low heat until the rice is tender and the liquid absorbed. Add a little extra boiling water if the rice dries out before it is cooked.

6 Stir the green onions and parsley into the finished dish, reserving a little of the mixture to sprinkle over the jambalaya. Serve hot.

Spicy Rice Cakes

INGREDIENTS

Makes 16 cakes

1 garlic clove, crushed

½-inch piece fresh ginger, peeled and finely chopped

¼ teaspoon ground turmeric

1 teaspoon sugar

½ teaspoon salt

1 teaspoon chili sauce

2 teaspoons fish sauce or soy sauce

2 tablespoons chopped fresh cilantro

juice of ½ lime

generous ½ cup (dry-weight) long-grain rice, cooked

peanuts, chopped

⅔ cup vegetable oil, for deep-frying

fresh cilantro sprigs, to garnish

1 In a food processor, process the garlic, ginger and turmeric. Add the sugar, salt, chili and fish sauce, chopped cilantro and lime juice.

2 Add three-quarters of the cooked rice and process until smooth and sticky. Transfer to a mixing bowl and stir in the remainder of the rice. Wet your hands and shape into thumb-size balls.

3 Roll the balls in chopped peanuts to coat evenly. Then set aside until ready to cook and serve.

4 Heat the vegetable oil in a deep-frying pan. Prepare a tray lined with paper towels to drain the rice cakes. Deep-fry three cakes at a time until crisp and golden, remove with a slotted spoon, then drain on the paper towels before serving hot.

Red Rice Rissoles

INGREDIENTS

Serves 6

1 large red onion, chopped

1 red pepper, chopped

2 garlic cloves, crushed

1 red chili pepper, finely chopped

2 tablespoons olive oil

2 tablespoons butter

generous 1 cup risotto rice

4 cups vegetable stock

4 sun-dried tomatoes, chopped

2 tablespoons tomato paste

2 teaspoons dried oregano

3 tablespoons chopped fresh parsley

6 ounces sharp cheese, such as smoked Cheddar

1 egg, beaten

1 cup dried breadcrumbs

peanut oil, for deep frying

salt and freshly ground black pepper

1 Fry the onion, pepper, garlic and chili in the oil and butter for 5 minutes. Stir in the rice and fry for 2 minutes more.

2 Pour in the stock and add the sun-dried tomatoes, tomato paste, oregano and seasoning. Bring to a boil, stirring occasionally, then cover and simmer for 20 minutes.

3 Stir in the parsley then transfer to a shallow dish and chill until firm. Divide the chilled rice into 12 equal portions and shape into balls.

4 Cut the cheese into 12 pieces and press a nugget into the center of each rice rissole.

5 Put the beaten egg in one bowl and the breadcrumbs in another. Dip the rissoles first into the egg, then into the breadcrumbs, coating each of them evenly.

6 Chill the rissoles for 30 minutes. Fill a deep-frying pan one-third full of oil and heat. Test with a cube of day-old bread; it should turn brown in less than a minute.

7 Fry the rissoles in batches for 3–4 minutes, reheating the oil in between. Drain on paper towels and keep warm, uncovered. Serve with a side salad.

Persian Rice with a Tahdeeg

Persian, or Iranian, cuisine is exotic and delicious, and the flavors are intense. A *tahdeeg* is the glorious, golden rice crust or "dig" that forms on the base of the saucepan.

INGREDIENTS

Serves 8

generous 2¼ cups basmati rice, rinsed thoroughly and soaked
2 garlic cloves, crushed
2 onions, 1 chopped, 1 thinly sliced
⅔ cup sunflower oil
⅔ cup green lentils, soaked
2½ cups stock
½ cup raisins
2 teaspoons ground coriander
3 tablespoons tomato paste
a few saffron strands
1 egg yolk, beaten
2 teaspoons plain yogurt
6 tablespoons butter, melted and strained
extra oil, for frying
salt and freshly ground black pepper

1 Drain the soaked rice, then cook it in plenty of boiling salted water for 3 minutes. Drain again.

2 In a large pan, fry the garlic and chopped onion in 2 tablespoons of the oil for 5 minutes. Add the lentils, stock, raisins, coriander, tomato paste and salt and pepper. Bring to a boil; simmer, covered, for 20 minutes.

3 Soak the saffron strands in a little hot water. Remove about ½ cup of the cooked rice and mix with the egg yolk and yogurt. Season well.

4 In a large saucepan, heat about two-thirds of the remaining oil and scatter the egg and yogurt rice evenly over the base.

5 Scatter the remaining rice into the pan, alternating it with the lentil mixture. Build up in a pyramid shape away from the sides of the pan, finishing with plain rice on top.

6 With a long wooden spoon handle, make three holes down to the base of the pan and drizzle over the butter. Bring to a high heat, then wrap the pan lid in a clean, wet dish towel and place firmly on top. When a good head of steam appears, turn the heat down to low. Cook for about 30 minutes.

7 Meanwhile, fry the sliced onion in the remaining oil until browned and crisp. Drain well and set aside.

8 Remove the rice pan from the heat, still covered, and stand it briefly in a sink of cold water for a minute or two to loosen the base. Remove the lid and mix a few spoons of the white rice with the saffron water.

9 Toss the rice and lentils together in the pan and spoon out onto a serving dish in a mound. Scatter the saffron rice on top. Break up the rice crust on the pan base and place pieces of it around the mound. Sprinkle with the fried onions and serve.

Festive Rice

This Thai dish is traditionally served shaped into a cone and surrounded by a variety of accompaniments.

INGREDIENTS

Serves 8

generous 2¼ cups Thai fragrant rice
4 tablespoons vegetable oil
2 garlic cloves, crushed
2 onions, finely sliced
2-inch piece fresh turmeric, peeled and crushed
3 cups water
1 can (14 ounces) unsweetened coconut milk
1–2 lemongrass stems, bruised

For the accompaniments

omelette strips
2 fresh red chili peppers, shredded
cucumber chunks
tomato wedges
deep-fried onions
prawn crackers

1 Wash the rice in several changes of water. Drain well.

2 Heat the oil in a wok and gently fry the garlic, onions and turmeric for a few minutes, until they are softened but not browned.

3 Add the rice and stir well so that each grain is thoroughly coated. Pour in the water and coconut milk and add the lemongrass.

4 Bring to a boil, stirring well. Cover the pan and cook gently for 15–20 minutes, or until the liquid has been completely absorbed.

5 Remove the pan from the heat. Cover with a clean dish towel, put on the lid and leave to stand in a warm place for 15 minutes.

6 Remove the lemongrass, turn out onto a serving platter and garnish the dish with the accompaniments.

Indian Pilau Rice

INGREDIENTS

Serves 4

generous 1 cup basmati rice, rinsed
    well
2 tablespoons vegetable oil
1 small onion, finely chopped
1 garlic clove, crushed
1 teaspoon fennel seeds
1 tablespoon sesame seeds
½ teaspoon ground turmeric
1 teaspoon ground cumin
½ teaspoon salt
2 whole cloves
4 green cardamom pods,
    lightly crushed
5 black peppercorns
scant 2 cups vegetable stock
1 tablespoon ground almonds
fresh cilantro sprigs, to garnish

1 Soak the rice in water for 30 minutes. Heat the oil in a saucepan, add the onion and garlic, and fry gently for 5–6 minutes, until softened.

2 Stir in the fennel and sesame seeds, the turmeric, cumin, salt, cloves, cardamom pods and peppercorns and fry for about 1 minute. Drain the rice well, add it to the pan and stir-fry for 3 minutes more.

3 Pour in the vegetable stock. Bring to a boil, then•cover, reduce the heat to very low and simmer gently for 20 minutes, without removing the lid, until all the liquid has been absorbed.

4 Remove from the heat and leave to stand for 2–3 minutes. Fluff the rice and stir in the ground almonds. Garnish the rice with cilantro sprigs.

Okra Fried Rice

Sliced okra gives a wonderful creamy texture to this delicious, simple dish.

INGREDIENTS

Serves 3–4

2 tablespoons vegetable oil
1 tablespoon butter or margarine
1 garlic clove, crushed
½ red onion, finely chopped
4 ounces okra, trimmed
2 tablespoons diced green and
    red bell peppers
½ teaspoon dried thyme
2 green chili peppers, finely chopped
½ teaspoon five-spice powder
1 vegetable stock cube
2 tablespoons soy sauce
1 tablespoon chopped fresh cilantro
3 cups cooked rice
salt and freshly ground black pepper
fresh cilantro sprigs, to garnish

1 Heat the oil and butter in a frying pan, add the garlic and onion and cook over medium heat for 5 minutes, until soft.

2 Thinly slice the okra, add to the frying pan and stir-fry gently for 6–7 minutes longer.

3 Add the bell peppers, thyme, chili peppers and five-spice powder and cook for 3 minutes, then crumble in the stock cube.

4 Add the soy sauce, chopped cilantro and rice. Heat through, stirring constantly. Season with salt and pepper. Garnish with cilantro sprigs.

Pistachio Pilaf

Saffron and ginger are traditional spices to add to rice dishes and they are delicious when mixed with fresh pistachios.

INGREDIENTS

Serves 4

3 onions
4 tablespoons olive oil
2 garlic cloves, crushed
1-inch piece fresh ginger, grated
1 green chili pepper, chopped
2 carrots, coarsely grated
generous 1 cup basmati rice, rinsed
¼ teaspoon saffron strands, crushed
scant 2 cups vegetable stock
2-inch cinnamon stick
1 teaspoon ground coriander
¼ cup fresh pistachios
1 pound fresh leaf spinach
1 teaspoon garam masala
fresh tomato salad, to serve
salt and freshly ground black pepper

1 Roughly chop two of the onions. Heat half the oil in a large saucepan and fry the onion with half the garlic, the ginger and the chili for 5 minutes until softened.

2 Mix in the carrots and rice, cook for 1 more minute and add the saffron, stock, cinnamon and coriander. Season well. Bring to a boil, then cover and simmer gently for 10 minutes without lifting the lid.

3 Remove from the heat and let stand, uncovered, for 5 minutes. Add the pistachios and mix them in with a fork. Remove the cinnamon stick and keep the rice warm.

4 Thinly slice the third onion and fry in the remaining oil for about 3 minutes. Stir in the spinach. Cover and cook for another 2 minutes.

5 Add the garam masala. Cook for a few minutes, then drain and roughly chop the spinach.

6 Spoon the spinach around the edge of a round serving dish and pile the pilaf in the center. Serve immediately with a tomato salad.

Basmati and Nut Pilaf

Use whatever nuts are your favorite in this dish – even unsalted peanuts are good, although almonds, cashew nuts or pistachios are more exotic.

INGREDIENTS

Serves 4–6

generous 1 cup basmati rice
1 onion, chopped
1 garlic clove, crushed
1 large carrot, coarsely grated
1–2 tablespoons sunflower oil
1 teaspoon cumin seeds
2 teaspoons ground coriander
2 teaspoons black mustard seeds
   (optional)
4 green cardamom pods
scant 2 cups vegetable stock or water
1 bay leaf
½ cup unsalted nuts
salt and freshly ground black pepper
chopped fresh parsley or cilantro,
   to garnish

1 Wash the rice in a sieve under cold running water. If there is time, soak the rice for 30 minutes, then drain it well in a sieve.

3 Stir in the rice and spices and cook for another 1–2 minutes, so that the grains are coated in oil.

6 If the rice is cooked, there will be small steam holes in the center of the pan. Discard the bay leaf and the cardamom pods.

2 In a large shallow frying pan, gently fry the onion, garlic and carrot in the oil for 3–4 minutes.

4 Pour in the stock or water, add the bay leaf and season well. Bring to a boil, cover and simmer very gently.

5 Remove from the heat without lifting the lid. Let stand on one side for about 5 minutes.

7 Stir in the nuts and check the seasoning. Sprinkle with the chopped parsley or cilantro.

Coconut Rice

This is a very popular way of cooking rice throughout the whole of South-east Asia. *Nasi Uduk* makes a wonderful accompaniment to any dish, and goes particularly well with fish, chicken and pork.

INGREDIENTS

Serves 4–6
1⅞ cups Thai fragrant rice
14-fluid ounce can coconut milk
1¼ cups water
½ teaspoon ground coriander
1 cinnamon stick
1 lemon grass stem, bruised
1 *pandan* or bay leaf (optional)
salt
Deep-fried Onions, to garnish

1 Wash the rice in several changes of water and then put in a pan with the coconut milk, water, coriander, cinnamon stick, lemon grass and *pandan* or bay leaf, if using, and salt. Bring to a boil, stirring to prevent the rice from settling on the bottom of the pan. Cover and cook over a very low heat for 12–15 minutes, or until all the coconut milk has been absorbed.

2 Fork the rice through carefully and remove the cinnamon stick, lemon grass and *pandan* or bay leaf. Cover the pan with a tight-fitting lid and then cook over the lowest possible heat for another 3–5 minutes.

3 Pile the rice onto a warm serving dish and serve garnished with the crisp Deep-fried Onions.

Spicy Rice with Chicken

This is a dish that is popular all over the East, in countries such as Indonesia. It is often served as sustaining breakfast fare. Hearty eaters tuck into a feast of spicy rice with chicken, and add shrimp, deep-fried onions, garlic and strips of fresh red and green chili. This is topped with a lightly fried egg and garnished with celery leaves.

INGREDIENTS

Serves 6
2¼-pound chicken, cut in 4 pieces, or
    4 chicken quarters
7½ cups water
1 large onion, quartered
1 inch fresh ginger root, peeled, halved
    and bruised
1⅞ cups Thai fragrant rice, rinsed
salt and freshly ground black pepper

1 Place the chicken pieces in a large pan with the water, onion quarters and ginger. Add seasoning, bring to a boil and simmer for 45–50 minutes, until the chicken is tender. Remove from the heat. Lift out the chicken, remove the meat and discard the skin and bones. Cut the chicken into bite-size pieces. Reserve the stock.

2 Strain the chicken stock into a clean pan and make it up to 7½ cups with water.

3 Add the rinsed rice to the chicken stock and stir continuously until it comes to a boil, to prevent the rice from settling on the bottom of the pan. Simmer gently for 20 minutes, without a lid. Stir, cover and cook the rice for 20 minutes more, stirring from time to time until the rice is soft and rather like a creamy risotto.

4 Stir the chicken pieces into the porridge and heat through for 5 minutes. Serve as it is, or with any of the garnishes and accompaniments suggested in the introduction.

Sushi

Ingredients

Makes 8–10

Tuna sushi

3 sheets nori (paper-thin seaweed)
5 ounces very-fresh tuna fillet, cut
  into strips
1 teaspoon wasabi paste
6 young carrots, blanched
6 cups cooked Japanese rice

Salmon sushi

2 eggs
½ teaspoon salt
2 teaspoons sugar
5 sheets nori
6 cups cooked Japanese rice
5 ounces very-fresh salmon fillet, cut
  into fingers
1 teaspoon wasabi paste
½ small cucumber, cut into strips

1 To make the tuna sushi, spread half a sheet of nori onto a bamboo mat, lay strips of tuna across the full length and season with the thinned wasabi. Place a line of blanched carrot next to the tuna and roll tightly. Moisten the edge with water and seal.

2 Place a square of damp waxed paper on the bamboo mat, then spread evenly with sushi rice. Place the non-wrapped tuna along the center and wrap tightly, enclosing the nori completely. Remove the paper and cut into neat rounds with a wet knife.

3 To make the salmon sushi, make a simple flat omelette by beating together the eggs, salt and sugar. Heat a large non-stick pan, pour in the egg mixture, stir briefly and allow to set. Transfer to a clean dish towel and cool.

4 Place the nori on a bamboo mat, cover with the omelette and trim to size. Spread a layer of rice over the omelette, then lay strips of salmon across the width. Season the salmon with the thinned wasabi, then place a strip of cucumber next to the salmon. Fold the bamboo mat in half. Cut into neat rounds with a wet knife.

Green Beans, Rice and Beef

INGREDIENTS

Serves 4

2 tablespoons butter or margarine
1 large onion, chopped
1 pound stewing beef, cubed
2 garlic cloves, crushed
1 teaspoon ground cinnamon
1 teaspoon ground cumin
1 teaspoon ground turmeric
1 pound tomatoes, chopped
2 tablespoons tomato paste
1½ cups water
2½ cups green beans, trimmed
  and halved
salt and freshly ground black pepper

For the rice

scant 1½ cups basmati rice, soaked in
  salted water for 2 hours
7½ cups water
3 tablespoons melted butter
2–3 saffron strands, soaked in
  1 tablespoon boiling water
pinch of salt

1 Melt the butter or margarine in a large saucepan or flameproof casserole and fry the onion until golden. Add the beef and fry until evenly browned, then add the garlic, spices, tomatoes, tomato paste and water. Season with salt and pepper. Bring to a boil, then simmer over low heat for about 30 minutes.

2 Add the green beans and continue cooking for another 15 minutes until the meat is tender and most of the meat juices have evaporated.

3 Meanwhile, prepare the rice. Drain, then boil it in salted water for about 5 minutes. Reduce the heat and simmer very gently for 10 minutes or until it is half-cooked. Drain, and rinse the rice in warm water. Wash and dry the saucepan.

4 Heat 1 tablespoon of the melted butter in the pan and stir in about a third of the rice. Spoon half of the meat mixture over the rice, add a layer of rice, then the remaining meat and finish with another layer of rice.

5 Pour the remaining melted butter over the rice and cover the pan with a clean dish towel. Secure with the lid and then steam the rice for 30–45 minutes over low heat.

6 Take 3 tablespoons of cooked rice from the pan and mix with the saffron water. Serve the cooked rice and beef on a large dish and sprinkle the saffron rice over the top.

Sweet and Sour Rice

Zereshk Polo is flavored with fruit and spices and is commonly served with chicken dishes.

INGREDIENTS

Serves 4
2 ounces *zereshk*
3 tablespoons melted butter
⅓ cup raisins
2 tablespoons sugar
1 teaspoon ground cinnamon
1 teaspoon ground cumin
scant 2 cups basmati rice, soaked in
    salted water for 2 hours
2–3 saffron strands, soaked in
    1 tablespoon boiling water
salt

1 Thoroughly wash the *zereshk* in cold water at least 4–5 times to rinse off any bits of grit.

2 Heat 1 tablespoon of the butter in a small frying pan and stir-fry the raisins for 1–2 minutes.

3 Add the *zereshk*, fry for a few seconds and then add the sugar, and half of the cinnamon and cumin. Cook briefly and then set aside.

4 Drain the rice and then boil in a saucepan in salted water for 5 minutes, reduce the heat and simmer for 10 minutes until half cooked.

5 Drain and rinse in lukewarm water and wash and dry the pan. Heat half of the remaining butter in the pan, add 1 tablespoon water and stir in half of the rice.

6 Sprinkle with half of the raisin and *zereshk* mixture and top with all but 3 tablespoons of the rice. Sprinkle over the remaining raisin mixture.

7 Blend the reserved rice with the remaining cinnamon and cumin and sprinkle over the top of the rice mixture. Drizzle the remaining butter over and then cover the pan with a clean dish towel and secure with a tightly fitting lid, lifting the corners of the cloth back over the lid. Steam the rice over a very low heat for about 30–40 minutes.

8 Just before serving, mix about 3 tablespoons of the rice with the saffron water. Spoon the rice on to a large flat serving dish and sprinkle the saffron rice over the top to decorate.

COOK'S TIP

Zereshk are very small dried berries that are delicious mixed with rice. They are available from most Persian and Middle Eastern food stores.

Bamie Goreng

This fried noodle dish is wonderfully accommodating. To the basic recipe you can add other vegetables, such as mushrooms, tiny pieces of chayote, broccoli, leeks or beansprouts, if you prefer. As with fried rice, you can use whatever you have to hand, bearing in mind the need to achieve a balance of colors, flavors and textures.

INGREDIENTS

Serves 6–8

1 pound dried egg noodles
1 boneless, skinless chicken breast
4 ounces pork loin
4 ounces calves' liver (optional)
2 eggs, beaten
6 tablespoons oil
1 ounce butter or margarine
2 garlic cloves, crushed
4 ounces cooked, peeled shrimp
4 ounces spinach or Chinese cabbage
2 celery stalks, finely sliced
4 scallions, shredded
about 4 tablespoons chicken broth
dark soy sauce and light soy sauce
salt and ground black pepper
deep-fried onions and celery leaves, to
    garnish

2 Finely slice the chicken, pork loin and calves' liver, if using.

4 Heat the remaining oil in a wok and fry the garlic with the chicken, pork and liver for 2–3 minutes, until they have changed color. Add the shrimp, spinach or Chinese cabbage, celery and scallions, tossing well.

5 Add the cooked and drained noodles and toss well again so that all the ingredients are well mixed. Add enough broth just to moisten and dark and light soy sauce to taste. Finally, stir in the scrambled eggs.

1 Cook the noodles in salted, boiling water for 3–4 minutes. Drain, rinse with cold water and drain again. Set aside until required.

3 Season the eggs. Heat 1 teaspoon oil with the butter or margarine in a small pan until melted and then stir in the eggs and keep stirring until scrambled. Set aside.

6 Serve, garnished with deep-fried onions and celery leaves.

Rice with Dill and Spicy Beans

This spiced rice dish is a favorite in Iran, where it is known as *Baghali Polo*.

INGREDIENTS

Serves 4

scant 1½ cups basmati rice, soaked in
   salted water for 3 hours
3 tablespoons melted butter
1½ cups shelled fava beans, fresh or
   frozen
6 tablespoons finely chopped fresh dill
1 teaspoon ground cinnamon
1 teaspoon ground cumin
2–3 saffron strands, soaked in
   1 tablespoon boiling water
salt

1 Drain the rice and then boil it in fresh salted water for 5 minutes. Reduce the heat and simmer very gently for 10 minutes. Drain and rinse in warm water.

2 Put 1 tablespoon of the butter in a non-stick saucepan and add enough rice to cover the base. Add a quarter of the beans and a little dill.

3 Add another layer of rice, then a layer of beans and dill and continue layering until all the beans and dill are used up, finishing with a layer of rice. Cook over low heat for 10 minutes.

4 Pour the remaining melted butter over the rice. Sprinkle with the cinnamon and cumin. Cover the pan with a clean dish towel and secure with a tight-fitting lid, lifting the corners of the cloth back over the lid. Steam over low heat for 30–45 minutes.

5 Mix 3 tablespoons of the rice with the saffron water. Spoon the remaining rice onto a large serving plate and sprinkle with the saffron-flavored rice to decorate. Serve with either a lamb or chicken dish.

COOK'S TIP

Saffron may seem expensive, however you need only a little to add flavor and color to a variety of savory and sweet dishes. And, as long as it is kept dry and dark, it never goes stale.

Mexican-style Rice

INGREDIENTS

Serves 6

1³/₄ cups long-grain white rice
1 onion, chopped
2 garlic cloves, chopped
1 pound tomatoes, peeled, seeded and
    coarsely chopped
4 tablespoons corn or peanut oil
3³/₄ cups chicken stock
4–6 small red chilies, such
    as *habaneros*
1 cup cooked green peas
salt and freshly ground black pepper
fresh cilantro sprigs, to garnish

1 Soak the rice in a bowl of hot
water for 15 minutes. Drain, rinse
well under cold running water, drain
again and set aside.

2 Combine the onion, garlic and
tomatoes in a food processor and
process to a purée.

3 Heat the oil in a large frying pan.
Add the drained rice and sauté
until it is golden brown. Using a slotted
spoon, transfer the rice to a saucepan.

4 Reheat the oil remaining in the
pan and cook the tomato purée for
2–3 minutes. Add it to the saucepan
and pour in the stock. Season to taste.
Bring to a boil, reduce the heat to the
lowest possible setting, cover the pan,
and cook for 15–20 minutes, until
almost all the liquid has been absorbed.
Slice the red chilies from tip to stem
end into four or five sections. Place in
a bowl of iced water until they curl
back to form flowers, then drain.

5 Stir the peas into the rice mixture
and cook, without a lid, until all
the liquid has been absorbed and the
rice is tender. Stir the mixture from
time to time.

6 Transfer the rice to a serving dish
and garnish with the drained chili
flowers and sprigs of cilantro. Warn
diners that these elaborate chili
"flowers" are blistering hot and
should be approached with caution.

Tossed Noodles with Seafood

INGREDIENTS

Serves 4–6

12 ounces thick egg noodles
4 tablespoons vegetable oil
3 slices fresh ginger, grated
2 garlic cloves, finely chopped
8 ounces mussels or clams
8 ounces raw shrimp, peeled
8 ounces squid, cut into rings
4 ounces oriental fish cake, sliced
1 red bell pepper, seeded and cut
    into rings
2 ounces sugar snap peas, ends
    removed
2 tablespoons soy sauce
½ teaspoon sugar
½ cup broth or water
1 tablespoon cornstarch
1–2 teaspoons sesame oil
salt and freshly ground black pepper
2 scallions, chopped, and 2 red chilies,
    seeded and chopped, to garnish

1 Cook the noodles in a large saucepan of boiling water until just tender. Drain, rinse under cold water, and drain well.

2 Heat the oil in a wok or large frying pan. Fry the ginger and garlic for 30 seconds. Add the mussels or clams, shrimp and squid, and stir-fry for about 4–5 minutes until the seafood changes color. Add the fish cake slices, bell pepper rings and sugar snap peas, and stir well.

3 In a bowl, mix the soy sauce, sugar, broth or water and cornstarch. Stir into the seafood, and bring to a boil. Add the noodles, and cook until they are heated through.

4 Add the sesame oil to the wok or pan, and season with salt and pepper to taste. Serve at once, garnished with the chopped scallions and red chilies.

Noodles with Spicy Meat Sauce

INGREDIENTS

Serves 4–6

2 tablespoons vegetable oil
2 dried red chilies, chopped
1 teaspoon grated fresh ginger
2 garlic cloves, finely chopped
1 tablespoon chili black bean paste
1 pound minced pork or beef
1 pound broad flat egg noodles
1 tablespoon sesame oil
2 scallions, chopped, to garnish

For the sauce
¼ teaspoon salt
1 teaspoon sugar
1 tablespoon soy sauce
1 teaspoon mushroom ketchup
1 tablespoon cornstarch
1 cup chicken broth
1 teaspoon Shaohsing wine or
    dry sherry

1 Heat the vegetable oil in a large saucepan. Add the dried chilies, ginger and garlic. Fry until the garlic starts to color, then gradually stir in the chili black bean paste.

2 Add the minced pork or beef, breaking it up with a spatula or wooden spoon. Cook over a high heat until the minced meat changes color and any liquid has evaporated.

3 Mix all the sauce ingredients in a cup. Make a well in the center of the pork mixture. Pour in the sauce mixture, and stir together. Simmer for 10–15 minutes until tender.

4 Meanwhile, cook the noodles in a large saucepan of boiling water for 5–7 minutes until just tender. Drain well, and toss with the sesame oil. Serve, topped with the meat sauce and garnished with the scallions.

Tomato Noodles with Fried Egg

INGREDIENTS

Serves 4

12 ounces medium-thick
  dried noodles
4 tablespoons vegetable oil
2 garlic cloves, very finely chopped
4 shallots, chopped
½ teaspoon chili powder
1 teaspoon paprika
2 carrots, finely diced
4 ounces button mushrooms,
  quartered
2 ounces peas
1 tablespoon tomato ketchup
2 teaspoons tomato paste
salt and freshly ground black pepper
butter for frying
4 eggs

1 Cook the noodles in a saucepan of boiling water until just tender. Drain, rinse under cold running water, and drain well.

2 Heat the oil in a wok or large frying pan. Add the garlic, shallots, chili powder and paprika. Stir-fry for about 1 minute, then add the carrots, mushrooms and peas. Continue to stir-fry until the vegetables are cooked.

3 Stir the tomato ketchup and paste into the vegetable mixture. Add the noodles, and cook over a medium heat until the noodles are heated through and have taken on the reddish tinge of the paprika and tomato.

4 Meanwhile, melt the butter in a frying pan, and fry the eggs. Season the noodle mixture, divide it among four serving plates, and top each portion with a fried egg.

Curry Fried Noodles

On its own, bean curd (tofu) has a fairly bland flavor, but it takes on the flavor of the curry spices wonderfully.

INGREDIENTS

Serves 4

4 tablespoons vegetable oil
2–3 tablespoons curry paste
8 ounces smoked bean curd, cut into
  1-inch cubes
8 ounces green beans, cut into
  1-inch lengths
1 red bell pepper, seeded and cut into
  fine strips
12 ounces rice vermicelli, soaked in
  warm water until soft
1 tablespoon soy sauce
salt and freshly ground black pepper
2 scallions, finely sliced, 2 red chilies,
  seeded and chopped, and 1 lime, cut
  into wedges, to garnish

1 Heat half the oil in a wok or large frying pan. Add the curry paste, and stir-fry for a few minutes, then add the bean curd. Continue to fry until golden brown. Using a slotted spoon, remove the cubes from the pan. Set aside until required.

2 Add the remaining oil to the wok or pan. When hot, add the green beans and red pepper. Stir-fry until the vegetables are cooked. You may need to moisten them with a little water.

3 Drain the noodles, and add them to the wok or frying pan. Continue to stir-fry until the noodles are heated through, then return the curried bean curd to the wok. Season with soy sauce, salt and pepper.

4 Transfer the mixture to a serving dish. Sprinkle with the scallions and chilies, and serve the lime wedges on the side.

Penne with Chili and Broccoli

INGREDIENTS

Serves 4

3 cups penne
1 pound small broccoli florets
2 tablespoons stock
1 garlic clove, crushed
1 small red chili pepper, sliced, or
  ½ teaspoon chili sauce
4 tablespoons plain yogurt
2 tablespoons toasted pine nuts
  or cashews
salt and ground black pepper

——— VARIATION ———

Green chilies can be used instead of red chilies and toasted almonds make a good substitute for pine nuts.

1 Add the pasta to a large pan of lightly salted boiling water and return to the boil. Place the broccoli in a steamer basket over the top. Cover and cook for 8–10 minutes until both are just tender. Drain.

2 Heat the stock and add the crushed garlic and chili or chili sauce. Stir over low heat for 2–3 minutes.

3 Stir in the broccoli, pasta and yogurt. Adjust the seasoning, sprinkle with nuts and serve hot.

Crisp Fried Rice Vermicelli

Mee Krob is usually served at celebratory meals. It is a crisp tangle of fried rice vermicelli, which is tossed in a piquant, garlic, sweet-and-sour sauce.

INGREDIENTS

Serves 4–6

oil for frying
6 ounces rice vermicelli
1 tablespoon chopped garlic
4–6 dried chilies, seeded and chopped
2 tablespoons chopped shallot
1 tablespoon dried shrimp, rinsed
4 ounces ground pork
4 ounces cooked shelled shrimp, chopped
2 tablespoons brown bean sauce
2 tablespoons rice wine vinegar
3 tablespoons fish sauce
3 tablespoons palm sugar
2 tablespoons tamarind or lime juice
½ cup bean sprouts

For the garnish
2 scallions, shredded
2 tablespoons fresh cilantro leaves
2 heads pickled garlic (optional)
2-egg omelet, rolled and sliced
2 red chilies, chopped

1 Heat the oil in a wok. Break the rice vermicelli apart into small handfuls about 3 inches long. Deep-fry in the hot oil until they puff up. Remove and drain on paper towels.

2 Leave 2 tablespoons of the hot oil in the wok, add the garlic, chilies, shallots and shrimp. Fry until fragrant.

3 Add the ground pork and stir-fry for about 3–4 minutes, until it is no longer pink. Add the shrimp and fry for 2 minutes more. Remove the mixture and set aside.

4 To the same wok, add the brown bean sauce, vinegar, fish sauce and palm sugar. Bring to a gentle boil, stir to dissolve the sugar and cook until thick and syrupy.

5 Add the tamarind or lime juice and adjust the seasoning. It should be sweet, sour and salty.

6 Reduce the heat. Add the pork and shrimp mixture and the bean sprouts to the sauce. Stir to mix.

7 Add the rice noodles and toss gently to coat them with the sauce, without breaking the noodles too much. Transfer the noodles to a platter. Garnish with scallions, cilantro leaves, pickled garlic, omelet strips and chilies.

Vegetarian Fried Noodles

When making this dish for non-vegetarians, or for vegetarians who eat fish, add a piece of *blacan* (compressed shrimp paste). A small chunk about the size of a bouillon cube, mashed with the chili paste, will add a deliciously rich, aromatic flavor.

INGREDIENTS

Serves 4

2 eggs
1 teaspoon chili powder
1 teaspoon turmeric
4 tablespoons vegetable oil
1 large onion, finely sliced
2 red chilies, seeded and
    finely sliced
1 tablespoon soy sauce
2 large cooked potatoes, cut into
    small cubes
6 pieces fried bean curd (tofu), sliced
8 ounces bean sprouts
4 ounces green beans, blanched
12 ounces fresh thick egg noodles
salt and freshly ground black pepper
sliced scallions, to garnish

1 Beat the eggs lightly, then strain them into a bowl. Heat a lightly greased omelet pan. Pour in half of the egg to cover the bottom of the pan thinly. When the egg is just set, turn the omelet over, and fry the other side briefly. Slide onto a plate, blot with paper towels, roll up, and cut into narrow strips. Make a second omelet in the same way, and slice it. Set the omelet strips aside for the garnish.

--- COOK'S TIP ---

Fried bean curd can be found in the refrigerated section of most good Asian food markets. It will keep for several days after opening.

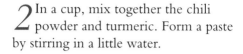

2 In a cup, mix together the chili powder and turmeric. Form a paste by stirring in a little water.

3 Heat the oil in a wok or large frying pan. Fry the onion until soft. Reduce the heat, and add the chili paste, sliced chilies and soy sauce. Fry for 2–3 minutes.

4 Add the potatoes, and fry for about 2 minutes, mixing well with the chilies. Add the bean curd, then the bean sprouts, green beans and noodles.

5 Gently stir-fry until the noodles are evenly coated and heated through. Take care not to break up the potatoes or the bean curd. Season with salt and pepper. Serve hot, garnished with the reserved omelet strips and scallion slices.

Thai Fried Noodles

Phat Thai has a fascinating flavor and texture. It's made with fine rice noodles and is considered one of the national dishes of Thailand.

INGREDIENTS

Serves 4–6
12 ounces rice noodles
3 tablespoons vegetable oil
1 tablespoon chopped garlic
16 uncooked jumbo shrimp, shelled,
   tails left intact, and deveined
2 eggs, lightly beaten
1 tablespoon dried shrimp, rinsed
2 tablespoons pickled white radish
2 ounces fried tofu, cut into
   small slivers
½ teaspoon dried chili flakes
4 ounces garlic chives, cut into
   2-inch lengths
1 cup bean sprouts
½ cup roasted peanuts, coarsely ground
1 teaspoon sugar
1 tablespoon dark soy sauce
2 tablespoons fish sauce
2 tablespoons tamarind juice
2 tablespoons cilantro leaves and
   1 kaffir lime, to garnish

1 Soak the noodles in warm water for 20–30 minutes, then drain.

2 Heat 1 tablespoon of the oil in a wok or large frying pan. Add the garlic and fry until golden. Stir in the shrimp and cook for about 1–2 minutes, until pink, tossing from time to time. Remove and set aside.

3 Heat another 1 tablespoon of oil in the wok. Add the eggs and tilt the wok to spread them into a thin sheet. Stir to scramble and break the eggs into small pieces. Remove from the wok and set aside with the shrimp.

4 Heat the remaining oil in the same wok. Add the dried shrimp, pickled radish, tofu and dried chilies. Stir briefly. Add the soaked noodles and stir-fry for 5 minutes.

5 Add the garlic chives, half the bean sprouts and half the peanuts. Season with the sugar, soy sauce, fish sauce and tamarind juice. Mix together well and cook until the noodles are completely heated through.

6 Return the shrimp and egg mixture to the wok and mix with the noodles. Serve garnished with the rest of the bean sprouts, peanuts, cilantro leaves and lime wedges.

Spicy Szechuan Noodles

INGREDIENTS

Serves 4

12 ounces thick noodles
6 ounces cooked chicken, shredded
2 ounces roasted cashews

For the dressing

4 scallions, chopped
2 tablespoons chopped cilantro
2 garlic cloves, chopped
2 tablespoons smooth peanut butter
2 tablespoons sweet chili sauce
1 tablespoon soy sauce
1 tablespoon sherry vinegar
1 tablespoon sesame oil
2 tablespoons olive oil
2 tablespoons chicken broth or water
10 toasted Szechuan peppercorns,
   ground

1 Cook the noodles in a saucepan of boiling water until just tender, following the directions on the package. Drain, rinse under cold running water, and drain well.

2 While the noodles are cooking, combine all the ingredients for the dressing in a large bowl. Whisk together well.

3 Add the noodles, shredded chicken and cashews to the dressing, toss gently to coat, and adjust the seasoning to taste. Serve at once.

— VARIATION —

For a change, you could substitute cooked turkey or pork for the chicken.

Sesame Noodles with Scallions

This simple, but very tasty, warm salad can be prepared and cooked in just a few minutes.

INGREDIENTS

Serves 4

2 garlic cloves, coarsely chopped
2 tablespoons Chinese sesame paste
1 tablespoon dark sesame oil
2 tablespoons soy sauce
2 tablespoons rice wine
1 tablespoon honey
pinch of five-spice powder
12 ounces soba or buckwheat noodles
4 scallions, finely sliced diagonally
2 ounces bean sprouts
3-inch piece of cucumber, cut
   into matchsticks
toasted sesame seeds
salt and freshly ground black pepper

1 Process the garlic, sesame paste, oil, soy sauce, rice wine, honey and five-spice powder with a pinch each of salt and pepper in a blender or food processor until smooth.

2 Cook the noodles in a saucepan of boiling water until just tender, following the directions on the package. Drain the noodles, and turn them into a bowl.

3 Toss the hot noodles with the dressing and the scallions. Top with the bean sprouts, cucumber and sesame seeds, and serve.

— COOK'S TIP —

If you can't find Chinese sesame paste, then use either tahini or smooth peanut butter instead.

SEARING-HOT SIDE DISHES, SALSAS AND RELISHES

Grilled meat, poultry or fish are delicious when spiced up with a red-hot salsa, chutney, relish or pickle. The selection varies from Coconut Chili Relish, which is pleasantly hot, to scorchingly hot Double Chili Salsa. Tomato and Onion Salad with red chili is surprisingly refreshing, and Pickled Cucumbers are good with cold meats or cheese.

Tomato and Onion Salad

A refreshing salad, *Atjar Ketimun,* which can be made ahead; it improves if well chilled before serving. Use firm, slightly under-ripe tomatoes so the flesh does not collapse when cut into dice.

INGREDIENTS

Serves 6

1 cucumber
3 tablespoons good-quality rice- or
   white-wine vinegar
2 teaspoons sugar
1 tomato, skinned, seeded and diced
1 small onion, finely sliced
1 fresh red chili, seeded and chopped
salt

1 Trim the ends from the cucumber. Peel it lengthwise but leave some of the skin on, to make the salad look more attractive. Cut it in thin slices and lay them out on a large plate. Sprinkle with a little salt and set aside for 15 minutes. Rinse well and dry.

2 Mix the vinegar, sugar and a pinch of salt together. Arrange all the vegetables in a bowl and pour over the vinegar, sugar and salt mixture. Cover the salad and chill before serving.

Coconut and Peanut Relish

The aroma of toasted coconut is wonderful and will immediately have you dreaming of warmer climes! *Serudeng* is served as an accompaniment to many Indonesian dishes; any leftovers can be stored in an airtight tin.

INGREDIENTS

Serves 6–8

14 ounces fresh coconut, grated, or
   dried coconut
1 cup salted peanuts
¼ teaspoon shrimp paste
1 small onion, quartered
2–3 garlic cloves, crushed
3 tablespoons oil
½ teaspoon tamarind pulp, soaked in
   2 tablespoons warm water
1 teaspoon coriander seeds, dry-fried
   and ground
½ teaspoon cumin seeds, dry-fried
   and ground
1 teaspoon dark brown sugar

1 Dry-fry the coconut in a wok or large frying pan over a medium heat, turning *all the time,* until it is crisp and a rich, golden color. Allow to cool and add half to the peanuts. Toss together to mix.

2 Grind the shrimp paste, with the onion and garlic, to a paste in a food processor or with a mortar and pestle. Fry in hot oil, without browning. Strain the tamarind and reserve the juice. Add the coriander, cumin, tamarind juice and brown sugar to the fried paste. Cook the mixture for 2–3 minutes, stirring constantly.

3 Stir in the remaining toasted coconut and let cool. When quite cold, mix with the peanut and coconut mixture.

Fiery Citrus Salsa

This very unusual salsa makes a fantastic marinade for all kinds of shellfish, and it is also delicious when drizzled over freshly barbecued meat.

INGREDIENTS

Serves 4
1 orange
1 green apple
2 fresh red chilies, halved and seeded
1 garlic clove
8 fresh mint leaves
juice of 1 lemon
salt and ground black pepper

1 Slice the bottom off the orange so that it stands firmly on a chopping board. Using a large, sharp knife, remove the peel by slicing from the top to the bottom of the orange.

2 Hold the orange in one hand over a bowl. Slice towards the middle of the fruit, to one side of a segment, and then gently twist the knife to ease the segment away from the membrane and out of the orange. Repeat to remove all the segments. Squeeze any juice from the remaining membrane.

3 Peel the apple, slice it into wedges and remove the core.

4 Place the chilies in a blender or food processor with the orange segments and juice, apple wedges, garlic and mint.

5 Process until smooth, then, with the motor running, pour in the lemon juice.

6 Season, pour into a bowl or small pitcher and serve immediately.

----- VARIATION -----

If you're feeling really fiery, don't seed the chilies! They will make the salsa particularly hot and fierce.

Salsa Verde

There are many versions of this classic green salsa. Serve this one with creamy mashed potato, or drizzled over the top of char-broiled squid.

INGREDIENTS

Serves 4

2–4 green chilies
8 scallions
2 garlic cloves
2 ounces salted capers
fresh tarragon sprig
1 bunch of fresh parsley
grated rind and juice of 1 lime
juice of 1 lemon
6 tablespoons olive oil
about 1 tablespoon green Tabasco,
   or to taste
ground black pepper

1 Halve the green chilies and remove their seeds. Trim the scallions and halve the garlic, then place in a food processor or blender. Pulse the power briefly until all the ingredients are coarsely chopped.

2 Use your fingertips to rub the excess salt off the capers, but do not rinse them. Add the capers, tarragon and parsley to the food processor or blender and pulse again until they are fairly finely chopped.

3 Transfer the mixture to a small bowl. Stir in the lime rind and juice, lemon juice and olive oil. Stir the mixture lightly so the citrus juice and oil do not emulsify.

4 Add green Tabasco and black pepper to taste. Chill until ready to serve but do not prepare more than 8 hours in advance.

VARIATION

If you can find only capers pickled in vinegar, they can be used for this salsa but they must be rinsed well in cold water first.

Berry Salsa

INGREDIENTS

Makes 3 cups

1 fresh jalapeño pepper
½ red onion, chopped
2 scallions, chopped
1 tomato, finely diced
1 small yellow bell pepper, seeded
   and chopped
4 tablespoons chopped fresh cilantro
¼ teaspoon salt
1 tablespoon raspberry vinegar
1 tablespoon fresh orange juice
1 teaspoon honey
1 tablespoon olive oil
1 cup strawberries, hulled
1 cup blueberries or blackberries
1 cup raspberries

1 Wearing rubber gloves, chop then finely grind the jalapeño pepper. Discard the seeds and membrane if a less hot flavor is desired. Place the jalapeño pepper in a bowl.

2 Add the red onion, scallions, tomato, pepper and cilantro, and stir to blend.

3 In a small mixing bowl, whisk together the salt, raspberry vinegar, orange juice, honey and olive oil. Pour this over the jalapeño mixture and stir well to combine.

4 Coarsely chop the strawberries. Add them to the jalapeño mixture with the blueberries or blackberries and the raspberries. Stir to blend together. Let stand at room temperature for about 3 hours.

5 Serve the salsa at room temperature, with broiled fish or poultry.

Mixed Vegetable Pickle

If you can obtain fresh turmeric, it makes such a difference to the color and appearance of *Acar Campur*. You can use almost any vegetable, bearing in mind that you need a balance of textures, flavors and colors.

INGREDIENTS

Makes 2–3 11-ounce jars

1 fresh red chili, seeded and sliced
1 onion, quartered
2 garlic cloves, crushed
½ teaspoon shrimp paste
4 macadamia nuts or 8 almonds
1 inch fresh turmeric, peeled and
   sliced, or 1 teaspoon ground turmeric
¼ cup sunflower oil
2 cups white vinegar
1 cup water
3–6 tablespoons granulated sugar
3 carrots
8 ounces green beans
1 small cauliflower
1 cucumber
8 ounces white cabbage
¾ cup dry-roasted peanuts,
   roughly crushed
salt

1 Place the chili, onion, garlic, shrimp paste, nuts and turmeric in a food processor and blend to a paste, or pound in a mortar with a pestle.

2 Heat the oil and stir-fry the paste to release the aroma. Add the vinegar, water, sugar and salt. Bring to a boil. Simmer for 10 minutes.

3 Cut the carrots into flower shapes. Cut the green beans into short, neat lengths. Separate the cauliflower into neat, bite-size florets. Peel and seed the cucumber and cut the flesh in neat, bite-size pieces. Cut the cabbage in neat, bite-size pieces.

4 Blanch each vegetable separately, in a large pan of boiling water, for 1 minute. Transfer to a colander and rinse with cold water, to halt the cooking. Drain well.

--- COOK'S TIP ---

This pickle is even better if you make it a few days ahead.

5 Add the vegetables to the sauce. Slowly bring to a boil and allow to cook for 5–10 minutes. Do not overcook – the vegetables should still be crunchy.

6 Add the peanuts and cool. Spoon into clean jars with lids.

Apricot Chutney

Chutneys can add zest to most meals, and in Pakistan you will usually find a selection of different kinds served in tiny bowls for people to choose from. Dried apricots are readily available from supermarkets or health food stores.

INGREDIENTS

Makes about 1 pound
3 cups dried apricots, finely chopped
1 teaspoon garam masala
1¼ cups light brown sugar
scant 2 cups malt vinegar
1 teaspoon ginger pulp
1 teaspoon salt
½ cup golden raisins
scant 2 cups water

1 Put all of the ingredients into a medium saucepan and mix them together thoroughly.

VARIATION

For a change, you could try dried peaches instead of the apricots. If desired, you can add heat with green chilies.

2 Bring the mixture to a boil, then turn down the heat and simmer for about 30–35 minutes, stirring occasionally as it cooks.

3 When the chutney has thickened to a fairly stiff consistency, transfer it to 2–3 clean jam jars and let cool thoroughly. This chutney should be covered tightly with a lid and stored in the fridge.

Tasty Toasts

These crunchy toasts have a wonderful spicy flavor. They make an ideal snack or part of a weekend brunch. They are especially delicious when served with freshly broiled tomatoes and baked beans.

INGREDIENTS

Serves 4
4 eggs
1¼ cups milk
2 fresh green chilies, finely chopped
2 tablespoons chopped fresh cilantro
¾ cup Cheddar or mozzarella cheese, grated
½ teaspoon salt
¼ teaspoon ground black pepper
4 slices bread
corn oil, for frying

1 Break the eggs into a medium bowl and whisk together. Slowly add the milk and whisk again. Add the green chilies, fresh cilantro, grated cheese and salt and pepper to taste.

2 Cut the bread slices in half diagonally, and soak them, one at a time, in the egg mixture.

3 Heat the corn oil in a medium frying pan, and fry the soaked bread slices over medium heat, turning them once or twice, until they are golden brown.

4 Drain off any excess oil as you remove the toasts from the pan and serve them immediately.

Double Chili Salsa

Only the very brave should attempt this scorchingly hot salsa! Spread it sparingly onto cooked meats and burgers.

INGREDIENTS

Serves 4–6

6 habanero chilies or Scotch bonnets
2 ripe tomatoes
4 standard green jalapeño chilies
2 tablespoons chopped fresh parsley
2 tablespoons olive oil
1 tablespoon balsamic or sherry vinegar
salt

— COOK'S TIP —

Habanero chilies, or Scotch bonnets, are among the hottest fresh chilies available. You may prefer to tone down the heat of this salsa by using a milder variety.

1 Skewer an habanero chili on a metal fork and hold it in a gas flame for 2–3 minutes, turning until the skin blackens and blisters. Repeat with all the chilies, then set aside.

2 Skewer and blister the tomatoes in the flame for 1–2 minutes, until the skin splits and wrinkles. Slip off the skins, halve the tomatoes, then use a teaspoon to scoop out and discard the seeds. Chop the flesh very finely.

3 Use a clean dish towel to rub the skins off the chilies.

4 Try not to touch the chilies with your bare hands: use a fork to hold them and slice them open with a sharp knife. Scrape out and discard the seeds, then finely chop the flesh.

5 Halve the jalapeño chilies, then remove their seeds and slice them finely widthwise into tiny strips. Mix together both types of chili, the tomatoes and the parsley.

6 Mix the olive oil, vinegar and a little salt, pour this over the salsa and cover the dish. The salsa will keep in the fridge for up to 3 days.

Piquant Pineapple Relish

This fruity sweet and sour pineapple relish is really excellent when it is served with crisply broiled chicken wings or bacon.

INGREDIENTS

Serves 4

14-ounce can crushed pineapple in
   natural juice
2 tablespoons light muscovado sugar
2 tablespoons wine vinegar
1 garlic clove
4 scallions
2 red chilies
10 fresh basil leaves
salt and ground black pepper

1 Drain the crushed pineapple pieces thoroughly and reserve about 4 tablespoons of the juice.

2 Place the juice in a small saucepan with the muscovado sugar and wine vinegar, then heat gently, stirring, until the sugar dissolves. Remove the pan from the heat and add salt and pepper to taste.

3 Finely chop the garlic and scallions. Halve the chilies, remove the seeds and finely chop them. Finely shred the basil.

4 Place the pineapple, garlic, scallions and chilies in a bowl. Mix well and pour in the sauce. Allow to cool for 5 minutes, then stir in the basil.

COOK'S TIP

This relish tastes extra special when made with fresh pineapple – substitute the juice of a freshly squeezed orange for the canned juice.

Pickled Cucumbers

Often served with salt beef, these gherkins or cucumbers are simple to prepare, but take a couple of days for the flavor to develop.

INGREDIENTS

Serves 6–8
6 small pickling cucumbers
5 tablespoons white wine vinegar
2 cups cold water
1 tablespoon salt
2 teaspoons sugar
10 black peppercorns
1 garlic clove
1 bunch fresh dill (optional)

1 You will need a large lidded jar or an oblong non-metallic container with a tightly fitting lid. Cut each cucumber lengthwise into six spears.

2 Mix together the wine vinegar, water, salt and sugar. Crush a few of the peppercorns and leave the rest whole. Add them to the liquid. Cut the garlic clove in half.

3 Arrange the cucumber spears in the jar or container, pour over the pickling liquid and add the garlic. Put in a few sprigs of dill, if using. Make sure they are completely submerged.

4 Leave the cucumbers, covered, in the fridge for at least two days. To serve, lift them out and discard the garlic, dill and peppercorns. Store any uneaten cucumbers in their pickling liquid in the fridge.

Spicy Fried Dumplins

Spicy Fried Dumplins are very easy to make. In the Caribbean, they are often served with saltfish or fried fish, but they can be eaten quite simply with butter and jam or cheese.

INGREDIENTS

Makes about 10

4 cups self-rising flour
2 teaspoons sugar
½ teaspoon ground cinnamon
pinch of grated nutmeg
½ teaspoon salt
1¼ cups milk
oil for frying

1 Sift the dry ingredients together into a large bowl, add the milk and mix and knead until smooth.

2 Divide the dough into ten balls, kneading each ball with floured hands. Press the balls gently to flatten into 3-inch rounds.

3 Heat a little oil in a nonstick frying pan until moderately hot. Place half the dumplings in the pan, reduce the heat to low and fry for about 15 minutes until they are golden brown, turning once.

4 Stand them on their sides for a few minutes to brown the edges, before removing them and draining on paper towels. Serve warm.

Kachumbali Salad

Kachumbali is a peppery relish from Tanzania, where it is served with grilled meat or fish dishes, together with rice – this salad uses the same combination of flavors.

INGREDIENTS

Serves 4–6
2 red onions
4 tomatoes
1 green chili
½ cucumber
1 carrot
juice of 1 lemon
salt and freshly ground black pepper

1 Slice the onions and tomatoes very thinly and place in a bowl.

2 Slice the chili lengthwise, discard the seeds, then chop very finely. Peel and slice the cucumber and carrot and add to the onions and tomatoes.

3 Squeeze the lemon juice over the salad. Season with salt and freshly ground black pepper and toss together to mix. Serve as an accompaniment, salad or relish.

— COOK'S TIP —

Traditional *Kachumbali* is made by very finely chopping the onions, tomatoes, cucumber and carrot which produces a very moist, sauce-like mixture. This is good served inside chappatis, and eaten as a salad roll.

Coconut Chili Relish

This simple but delicious relish is widely made in Tanzania. Only the white part of the coconut flesh is used.

INGREDIENTS

Makes about 2 ounces
2 ounces fresh or dried coconut
2 teaspoons lemon juice
¼ teaspoon salt
2 teaspoons water
¼ teaspoon finely chopped red chili

1 Grate the coconut and place in a mixing bowl. If using dried coconut, add just enough water to moisten.

2 Add the lemon juice, salt, water and chili. Stir thoroughly and serve as a relish with meats or as an accompaniment to a main dish.

Chili Bean Dip

This creamy and tangy dip is made from kidney beans blended with cheese and spices. It is best served warm with triangles of golden brown broiled pita bread or a generous helping of crunchy tortilla chips.

INGREDIENTS

Serves 4
2 garlic cloves
1 onion
2 fresh green chilies
2 tablespoons vegetable oil
1–2 teaspoons hot chili powder
14-ounce can kidney beans
3 ounces aged Cheddar cheese, grated
1 red chili, seeded
salt and ground black pepper

1 Finely chop the garlic and onion. Seed and finely chop the fresh green chilies.

2 Heat the oil in a frying pan and add the garlic, onion, green chilies and chili powder. Cook gently for 5 minutes, stirring regularly, until the onion is softened.

3 Drain the can of kidney beans, reserving the liquor. Blend all but 2 tablespoons of the beans to a paste in a food processor or blender.

4 Add the processed beans to the frying pan with 2–3 tablespoons of the reserved liquor. Heat gently, stirring to mix well.

5 Stir in the whole kidney beans and the grated Cheddar cheese. Cook gently for about 2–3 minutes, stirring until all the cheese melts. Add salt and plenty of freshly ground black pepper to taste.

6 Cut the fresh red chili into tiny strips. Spoon the dip into four individual serving bowls and sprinkle the chili strips over the top of each one. Serve warm.

COOK'S TIP

For a dip with a coarser texture, do not process the kidney beans in a food processor or blender; instead, mash them with a potato masher.

Chili Relish

This spicy tomato and red pepper relish will keep for at least a week in the fridge. Serve it with sausages and burgers in fresh white baps with a crisp salad.

INGREDIENTS

Serves 8

6 tomatoes
1 onion
1 red bell pepper, seeded
2 garlic cloves
2 tablespoons olive oil
1 teaspoon ground cinnamon
1 teaspoon chili flakes
1 teaspoon ground ginger
1 teaspoon salt
½ teaspoon ground black pepper
⅓ cup light muscovado sugar
5 tablespoons cider vinegar
1 handful of fresh basil leaves

COOK'S TIP

This relish thickens slightly on cooling so don't worry if the mixture seems a little wet at the end of step 5.

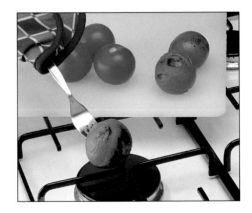

1 Skewer each of the tomatoes in turn on a metal fork and hold in a gas flame for 1–2 minutes, turning until the skin splits and wrinkles. Slip off the skins, then coarsely chop the tomatoes.

2 Coarsely chop the onion, red bell pepper and garlic. Heat the oil in a saucepan. Add the onion, red bell pepper and garlic.

3 Cook gently for 5–8 minutes, until the bell pepper is softened. Add the chopped tomatoes, cover and cook for 5 minutes, until the tomatoes release their juices.

4 Stir in the cinnamon, chili flakes, ginger, salt, pepper, sugar and vinegar. Bring gently to a boil, stirring until the sugar dissolves.

5 Simmer, uncovered, for about 20 minutes, or until the mixture is pulpy. Stir in the basil leaves and check the seasoning.

6 Allow the relish to cool completely, then transfer it to a glass jam jar or a plastic container with a tightly fitting lid. Store, covered, in the fridge.

Spiced Carrot Dip

This is a delicious low-fat dip with a sweet and spicy flavor. Serve wheat crackers or fiery tortilla chips as accompaniments for dipping.

INGREDIENTS

Serves 4

1 onion
3 carrots
grated rind and juice of 2 oranges
1 tablespoon hot curry paste
²/₃ cup low-fat plain yogurt
1 handful of fresh basil leaves
1–2 tablespoons fresh lemon juice,
  to taste
red Tabasco, to taste
salt and ground black pepper

1 Using a sharp vegetable knife, finely chop the onion. Peel and grate the carrots. Place the onion, carrots, orange rind and juice and hot curry paste in a small saucepan. Bring the mixture to a boil, cover with a lid and simmer for about 10 minutes, or until tender.

2 Process the mixture in a blender or food processor until smooth. Let cool completely.

3 Stir in the yogurt, then tear the basil leaves into small pieces and stir them into the carrot mixture.

4 Add lemon juice, Tabasco, salt and pepper to taste and serve.

COOK'S TIP

Use strained yogurt or sour cream instead of plain yogurt for a creamier dip.

Red Onion Raita

Raita is a traditional Indian accompaniment for most hot curries. It is also delicious when served with a pile of spicy poppadums as a dip.

INGREDIENTS

Serves 4

1 teaspoon cumin seeds
1 small garlic clove
1 small green chili, seeded
1 large red onion
²/₃ cup plain yogurt
2 tablespoons chopped fresh cilantro, plus extra to garnish
½ teaspoon sugar
salt

1 Heat a small frying pan and dry fry the cumin seeds for 1–2 minutes, until they release their aroma and begin to pop.

2 Lightly crush the cumin seeds in a mortar and pestle, or flatten them with the heel of a heavy-bladed knife until crushed.

3 Finely chop the garlic, green chili and red onion. Stir into the yogurt with the crushed cumin seeds and chopped cilantro.

4 Add sugar and salt to taste. Spoon the raita into a small bowl and chill until ready to serve. Garnish with extra cilantro before serving.

COOK'S TIP

For an extra tangy raita, stir in 1 tablespoon lemon juice.

SWEET AND SPICY DESSERTS AND CAKES

Warm spices, such as nutmeg, ginger, cinnamon and cardamom, are added to fresh fruit salads, ice creams, pastries, hot desserts and cakes. The selection ranges from Fresh Pineapple with Ginger to wickedly sweet spicy Baklava, from Cinnamon Rolls to Caribbean Fruit and Rum Cake, with an Egyptian version of Spiced Bread Pudding, and delicious spicy Caramel Rice Pudding.

Spicy Noodle Dessert

A traditional Jewish recipe, Spicy Noodle Dessert has a warm aromatic flavor and makes a delicious dessert.

INGREDIENTS

Serves 4–6
6 ounces wide egg noodles
1 cup cottage cheese
½ cup cream cheese
½ cup superfine sugar
2 eggs
½ cup sour cream
1 teaspoon vanilla extract
pinch of ground cinnamon
pinch of grated nutmeg
½ teaspoon grated lemon rind
4 tablespoons butter
¼ cup slivered almonds
½ cup fine dried white bread crumbs
confectioner's sugar for dusting

1 Preheat the oven to 350°F. Grease a shallow baking dish. Cook the noodles in a large saucepan of boiling water until just tender. Drain well.

2 Beat the cottage cheese, cream cheese and sugar together in a bowl. Add the eggs, one at a time, and stir in the sour cream. Stir in the vanilla extract, ground cinnamon, grated nutmeg and lemon rind.

3 Fold the noodles into the cheese mixture. Spoon into the prepared baking dish, and level the surface.

4 Melt the butter in a frying pan. Add the almonds, and fry for about 1 minute. Remove from the heat.

5 Stir in the bread crumbs, mixing well. Sprinkle the mixture over the pudding. Bake for 30–40 minutes or until the mixture is set. Serve hot, dusted with a little confectioner's sugar.

Avocado Salad in Ginger and Orange Sauce

This is an unusual fruit salad since avocado is more often treated as a vegetable. However, in the Caribbean it is used as a fruit, which of course it is!

INGREDIENTS

Serves 4
2 firm ripe avocados
3 firm ripe bananas, chopped
12 fresh cherries or strawberries
juice of 1 large orange
shredded fresh ginger

For the ginger syrup
2 ounces fresh ginger root, chopped
3¾ cups water
1 cup raw sugar
2 cloves

1 First make the ginger syrup; place the ginger, water, sugar and cloves in a saucepan and bring to a boil. Reduce the heat and simmer for about 1 hour, until well reduced and syrupy.

2 Remove the ginger and discard and set aside to cool. Store in a covered container in the fridge.

3 Peel the avocados, cut into cubes and place in a bowl with the bananas and cherries or strawberries.

4 Pour the orange juice over the fruits. Add 4 tablespoons of the ginger syrup and mix gently, using a metal spoon. Chill for 30 minutes and add a little shredded ginger.

Fresh Pineapple with Ginger

This refreshing dessert can also be made with canned pineapple. This makes a good substitute, but fresh is best.

INGREDIENTS

Serves 4

1 fresh pineapple, peeled
slivers of fresh coconut
1¼ cups pineapple juice
4 tablespoons coconut liqueur
1-inch piece preserved ginger, plus
   3 tablespoons of the syrup

1 Peel and slice the pineapple, arrange in a serving dish and sprinkle the coconut slivers on top.

2 Place the pineapple juice and coconut liqueur in a saucepan and heat gently.

3 Thinly slice the ginger and add to the pan along with the ginger syrup. Bring just to a boil and then simmer gently until the liquid is slightly reduced and the sauce is fairly thick.

4 Pour the sauce over the pineapple and coconut, let cool, then chill before serving.

COOK'S TIP

If fresh coconut is not available, then use dried coconut instead.

Spiced Nutty Bananas

Cinnamon and nutmeg are spices which perfectly complement bananas in this delectable dessert.

INGREDIENTS

Serves 3

6 ripe, but firm, bananas
2 tablespoons chopped unsalted cashew nuts
2 tablespoons chopped unsalted peanuts
2 tablespoons dried coconut
$\frac{1}{2}$–1 tablespoon raw sugar
1 teaspoon ground cinnamon
$\frac{1}{2}$ teaspoon freshly grated nutmeg
$\frac{2}{3}$ cup orange juice
4 tablespoons rum
1 tablespoon butter or margarine
heavy cream, to serve

1 Preheat the oven to 400°F. Slice the bananas and place in a greased, shallow ovenproof dish.

2 Mix together the cashew nuts, peanuts, coconut, sugar, cinnamon and nutmeg in a small bowl.

3 Pour the orange juice and rum over the bananas, then sprinkle with the nut and sugar mixture.

4 Dot the top with butter or margarine, then bake in the oven for 15–20 minutes or until the bananas are golden and the sauce is bubbly. Serve with heavy cream.

—— COOK'S TIP ——

Freshly grated nutmeg makes all the difference to this dish. More rum can be added if preferred. Chopped mixed nuts can be used instead of peanuts.

Fruits of the Tropics Salad

INGREDIENTS

Serves 4–6

1 medium pineapple
14-ounce can guava halves in syrup
2 medium bananas, sliced
1 large mango, peeled, pitted and diced
4 ounces preserved ginger and
  2 tablespoons of the syrup
4 tablespoons thick coconut milk
2 teaspoons sugar
½ teaspoon freshly grated nutmeg
½ teaspoon ground cinnamon
strips of coconut, to decorate

1 Peel, core and cube the pineapple, and place in a serving bowl. Drain the guavas, reserve the syrup and chop. Add the guavas to the bowl with one of the bananas and the mango.

2 Chop the preserved ginger and add to the pineapple mixture.

3 Pour 2 tablespoons of the ginger syrup, and the reserved guava syrup into a blender or food processor and add the other banana, the coconut milk and the sugar. Blend to make a smooth creamy purée.

4 Pour the banana and coconut mixture over the fruit, add a little grated nutmeg and a sprinkling of cinnamon. Serve chilled, decorated with strips of coconut.

Coconut and Nutmeg Ice Cream

An easy-to-make heavenly ice cream that will be loved by all for its tropical taste. Lemon balm an easily grown herb, gives it a spicy fragrance.

INGREDIENTS

Serves 8
14-ounce can evaporated milk
14-ounce can condensed milk
14-ounce can coconut milk
freshly grated nutmeg
1 teaspoon almond extract
lemon balm sprigs, lime slices and
    shredded coconut, to decorate

1 Mix together the evaporated, condensed and coconut milks in a large freezerproof bowl and stir in the nutmeg and almond extract.

2 Chill in a freezer for an hour or two until the mixture is semi-frozen.

3 Remove from the freezer and whisk the mixture with a hand or electric whisk until it is fluffy and almost doubled in volume.

4 Pour into a freezer container, then cover and freeze. Soften slightly before serving, decorated with lemon balm, lime slices and shredded coconut.

Baklava

This is queen of all pastries with its exotic flavors and is usually served for the Persian New Year on March 21, celebrating the first day of spring.

INGREDIENTS

Serves 6–8
3³/₄ cups ground
    pistachio nuts
1¹/₄ cups confectioner's sugar
1 tablespoon ground cardamom
about ²/₃ cup unsalted butter,
    melted
1 pound filo pastry

For the syrup
2 cups granulated or
    superfine sugar
1¹/₄ cups water
2 tablespoons rose water

1 First make the syrup: place the sugar and water in a saucepan, bring to a boil and then simmer for about 10 minutes until syrupy. Stir in the rose water and set aside to cool.

2 Mix together the pistachio nuts, confectioner's sugar and ground cardamom. Preheat the oven to 325°F and brush a large rectangular baking pan with a little melted butter.

3 Taking one sheet of filo pastry at a time, and keeping the remainder covered with a damp cloth, brush with melted butter and lay on the bottom of the pan. Continue until you have six buttered layers in the pan. Spread half of the nut mixture over, pressing down with a spoon.

4 Take another six sheets of filo pastry, brush each with butter and lay over the nut mixture. Sprinkle over the remaining nuts and top with a final layer of six filo sheets each brushed again with butter. Cut the pastry diagonally into small lozenge shapes using a sharp knife. Pour the remaining melted butter over the top.

5 Bake for 20 minutes, then increase the heat to 400°F and bake for about 15 minutes until light golden in color and puffed.

6 Remove from the oven and drizzle about three quarters of the syrup over the pastry, reserving the remainder for serving. Arrange the baklava lozenges on a large glass dish and serve with extra syrup.

Spiced Bread Pudding

Here's a spicy Egyptian version of bread and butter pudding.

INGREDIENTS

Serves 4

10–12 sheets filo pastry
2½ cups milk
1 cup heavy or whipping cream
1 egg, beaten
2 tablespoons rose water
½ cup each chopped pistachio nuts,
    almonds and hazelnuts
⅔ cup raisins
1 tablespoon ground cinnamon
light cream, to serve

1 Preheat the oven to 325°F. Bake the filo pastry, on a baking sheet, for 15–20 minutes until crisp. Remove the baking sheet from the oven and raise the temperature to 400°F.

2 Scald the milk and heavy or whipping cream by pouring into a pan and heating very gently until hot but not boiling. Slowly add the beaten egg and the rose water. Cook over a very low heat, until the mixture begins to thicken, stirring all the time.

3 Crumble the pastry using your hands and then spread in layers with the nuts and raisins into the bottom of a shallow baking dish.

4 Pour the custard mixture over the nut and pastry base and bake in the oven for 20 minutes until golden. Sprinkle with cinnamon and serve with light cream.

Caramel Rice Pudding

This rice pudding is delicious served with crunchy fresh fruit.

INGREDIENTS

Serves 4

4 tablespoons short grain
  pudding rice
5 tablespoons demerara sugar
1 teaspoon ground cinnamon
14-ounce can evaporated milk
  made up to 2½ cups
  with water
knob of butter
1 small fresh pineapple
2 crisp eating apples
2 teaspoons lemon juice

1 Preheat the oven to 300°F. Put the rice in a sieve and wash thoroughly under cold water. Drain well and put into a lightly greased soufflé dish.

2 Add 2 tablespoons sugar and the cinnamon to the dish. Add the diluted milk and stir gently.

3 Dot the surface of the rice with butter and bake for 2 hours, then let cool for 30 minutes.

4 Meanwhile, peel, core and slice the pineapple and apples and then cut the pineapple into chunks. Toss the fruit in lemon juice and set aside.

5 Preheat the broiler and sprinkle the remaining sugar over the rice. Broil for 5 minutes, or until the sugar has caramelized. Let the rice stand for 5 minutes to allow the caramel to harden, then serve with the fresh fruit.

Spiced Rice Pudding

Both Muslim and Hindu communities prepare this pudding, which is traditionally served at mosques and temples.

INGREDIENTS

Serves 4–6

1 tablespoon ghee or melted
  unsalted butter
2-inch cinnamon stick
1 cup light brown sugar
½ cup ground rice
5 cups milk
1 teaspoon ground cardamom
scant ½ cup golden raisins
¼ cup slivered almonds
½ teaspoon grated nutmeg, to serve

1 In a heavy pan, heat the ghee or butter and fry the cinnamon and sugar. Keep frying until the sugar begins to caramelize. Reduce the heat immediately when this happens.

2 Add the rice and half the milk. Bring to a boil, stirring constantly to prevent the milk from boiling over. Reduce the heat and simmer until the rice is cooked, stirring frequently.

3 Add the remaining milk, the cardamom, raisins and almonds and simmer, stirring constantly, to prevent the rice from sticking to the base of the pan. When the mixture has thickened, serve hot or cold, sprinkled with the grated nutmeg.

Date and Nut Pastries

INGREDIENTS

Makes 35–40
4 cups flour
1 cup unsalted butter, cut into cubes
3 tablespoons rose water
4–5 tablespoons milk
confectioner's sugar,
    for sprinkling

For the filling
1¼ cups dates, pitted
    and chopped
1¼ cups walnuts, finely
    chopped
¾ cup blanched almonds, finely
    chopped
½ cup pistachio nuts, finely
    chopped
½ cup water
½ cup granulated sugar
2 teaspoons ground cinnamon

1 Preheat the oven to 325°F. First make the filling: place the dates, walnuts, almonds, pistachio nuts, water, granulated sugar and cinnamon in a small saucepan and cook over a low heat until the dates are soft and the water has been absorbed.

2 Place the flour in a large bowl and add the butter, working it into the flour with your fingertips.

3 Add the rose water and milk and knead the dough until it's soft.

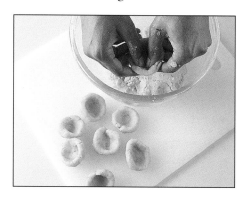

4 Take walnut-size lumps of dough. Roll each into a ball and hollow with your thumb. Pinch the sides.

5 Place a spoonful of date mixture in the hollow and then press the dough back over the filling to seal.

6 Arrange the pastries on a large baking tray. Press to flatten them slightly. Make little dents with a fork on the pastry. Bake in the oven for 20 minutes. Do not let them change color or the pastry will become hard. Cool slightly and then sprinkle with confectioner's sugar and serve.

Cinnamon Balls

Ground almonds or hazelnuts form the basis of most Passover cakes and biscuits. These balls should be soft inside, with a very strong cinnamon flavor. They harden with keeping, so it is a good idea to freeze some and use them only when required.

INGREDIENTS

Makes about 15
1 1/2 cups ground almonds
1/3 cup superfine sugar
1 tablespoon ground cinnamon
2 egg whites
oil, for greasing
confectioner's sugar, for dredging

1 Preheat the oven to 350°F. Lightly grease a large baking sheet with a little oil.

2 Mix together the ground almonds, sugar and cinnamon. Whisk the egg whites until they begin to stiffen and fold enough into the almonds to make a fairly firm mixture.

3 Wet your hands with cold water and roll small spoonfuls of the mixture into balls. Place these at intervals on the baking sheet.

4 Bake for about 15 minutes in the center of the oven. They should be slightly soft inside – too much cooking will make them hard and tough.

5 Slide a spatula under the balls to release them from the baking sheet and let cool. Sift a few tablespoons of confectioner's sugar on to a plate and when the cinnamon balls are cold slide them on to the plate. Shake gently to completely cover the cinnamon balls in sugar and store in an airtight container or in the freezer.

Apple and Cinnamon Crumble Cake

This fantastic cake has layers of spicy fruit and crumble and is quite delicious served warm with fresh cream.

INGREDIENTS

Makes 1 cake
3 large cooking apples
½ teaspoon ground cinnamon
1 cup butter
1¼ cups superfine sugar
4 eggs
4 cups self-rising flour

For the crumble topping
¾ cup raw sugar
1¼ cups all-purpose flour
1 teaspoon ground cinnamon
about 4½ tablespoons dried coconut
½ cup butter

1 Preheat the oven to 350°F. Grease a 10-inch round cake pan and line the base with wax paper. To make the crumble topping, mix together the sugar, flour, cinnamon and coconut in a bowl, then rub in the butter with your fingertips and set aside.

2 Peel and core the apples, then grate them coarsely. Place them in a bowl, sprinkle with the cinnamon and set aside.

3 Cream the butter and sugar in a bowl with an electric mixer, until light and fluffy. Beat in the eggs, one at a time, beating well after each addition.

4 Sift in half the flour, mix well, then add the remaining flour and stir until smooth.

5 Spread half the cake mixture evenly over the bottom of the prepared pan. Spoon the apples on top and sprinkle over half the crumble topping.

6 Spread the remaining cake mixture over the crumble and finally top with the remaining crumble topping.

7 Bake for 1 hour 10 minutes – 1 hour 20 minutes, covering the cake with foil if it browns too quickly. Leave in the pan for about 5 minutes before turning out onto a wire rack. Once cool, cut into slices to serve.

COOK'S TIP

To make the topping in a food processor, add all the ingredients and process for a few seconds until the mixture resembles bread crumbs. You can also grate the apples using the grating disk. If you don't have a 10-inch round pan you can use a 8-inch square cake pan.

Banana Ginger Cake

INGREDIENTS

Makes 1 cake

1²/₃ cups all-purpose flour
2 teaspoons baking soda
2 teaspoons ground ginger
1¼ cups medium oatmeal
4 tablespoons dark muscovado sugar
6 tablespoons sunflower margarine
³/₄ cup maple syrup
1 egg, beaten
3 ripe bananas, mashed
³/₄ cup confectioners' sugar
preserved ginger, to decorate

1 Preheat the oven to 325°F. Grease and line a 7 x 11-inch cake pan.

2 Stir together the flour, baking soda and ginger, then stir in the oatmeal. Mix the sugar, margarine and maple syrup in a saucepan, then stir into the flour mixture. Beat in the egg and mashed bananas.

3 Spoon into the pan and bake for about 1 hour, or until firm to the touch. Allow to cool in the pan, then turn out and cut into squares.

4 Sift the confectioners' sugar into a bowl and stir in just enough water to make a smooth, runny icing. Drizzle the icing over each square and top with a piece of preserved ginger.

COOK'S TIP

This is a nutritious, energy-giving cake that is a really good choice for packed lunches as it doesn't break up too easily.

Spiced Date and Walnut Cake

Mixed spice adds a warm flavor to this low-fat, high-fiber cake. Simply serve it on its own, or spread it with butter and honey for an extra special snack during the afternoon.

INGREDIENTS

Makes 1 cake
2½ cups whole wheat self-rising flour
2 teaspoons mixed spice
scant 1 cup chopped dates
½ cup chopped walnuts
4 tablespoons sunflower oil
½ cup dark muscovado sugar
1¼ cups skim milk
walnut halves, to decorate

— VARIATION —

Pecans can be used in place of the walnuts in this cake, if you like.

1 Preheat the oven to 350°F. Grease and line a 2-pound loaf pan with waxed paper.

2 Sift together the self-rising flour and mixed spice, adding back any bran from the sifter. Stir in the dates and walnuts.

3 Mix the oil, sugar and milk, then stir evenly into the dry ingredients. Spoon the mixture into the prepared loaf pan.

4 Arrange the walnut halves over the top of the cake mixture. Bake the cake for 45–50 minutes, or until golden brown and firm. Turn out the cake, remove the lining paper and let cool on a wire rack.

Cinnamon Rolls

INGREDIENTS

Makes 24 small rolls
For the dough
1²/₃ cups all-purpose flour
½ teaspoon salt
2 tablespoons sugar
1 teaspoon rapid-rise dried yeast
3 tablespoons oil
1 egg
½ cup warm milk
/₂ cup warm water

For the filling
2 tablespoons butter, softened
2 tablespoons dark brown sugar
½–1 teaspoon ground cinnamon
1 tablespoon raisins

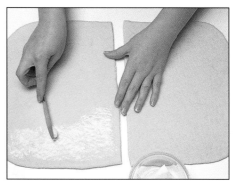

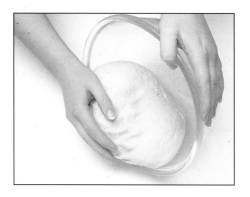

1 Sift the flour, salt, and sugar and sprinkle over the yeast. Mix the oil, egg, milk and water and add to the flour. Mix to a dough, then knead until smooth. Let rise until doubled in size and then punch it down again.

2 Roll out the dough into a large rectangle and cut in half vertically. Spread over the soft butter, reserving 1 tablespoon for brushing. Mix the sugar and cinnamon and sprinkle over the top. Dot with the raisins.

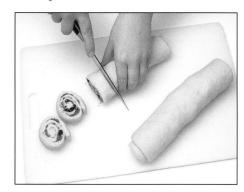

3 Roll each piece into a long Swiss roll shape, to enclose the filling. Cut into 1-inch slices, arrange flat on a greased baking sheet and brush with the remaining butter. Let rise again for about 30 minutes.

4 Preheat the oven to 400°F and bake the cinnamon rolls for about 20 minutes. Let cool on a wire rack. Serve fresh for breakfast or tea, with extra butter if liked.

Peach Kuchen

The joy of this cake is its all-in-one simplicity. It can be served straight from the oven, or cut into squares when cold.

INGREDIENTS

Serves 8
3 cups self-rising flour
1 cup superfine sugar
3/4 cup unsalted butter, softened
2 eggs
1/2 cup milk
6 large peeled peaches, sliced or
    1 pound plums or cherries, pitted
1/2 cup brown sugar
1/2 teaspoon ground cinnamon
sour cream, to serve (optional)

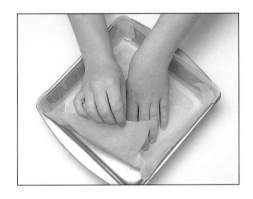

1 Preheat the oven to 375°F. Lightly grease and line a 8 x 10 x 1 inch cake pan.

2 Put the flour, sugar, butter, eggs and milk into a large bowl and beat for a few minutes, until you have a smooth batter. Spoon it into the prepared cake pan.

3 Arrange the peaches, plums or cherries over the cake mixture. Mix the brown sugar and cinnamon and sprinkle over the fruit.

--- COOK'S TIP ---

To peel ripe peaches, cover with boiling water for 20 seconds. The skin will then slip off easily.

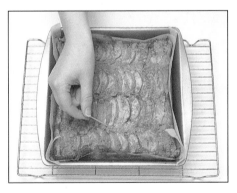

4 Bake for about 40 minutes, testing for doneness by inserting a toothpick in the center.

5 Serve the cake warm or cool with the sour cream, if you like.

Caribbean Fruit and Rum Cake

This is a delicious recipe for a cake that is eaten at Christmas, weddings and other special occasions. It is known as Black Cake, because, traditionally, the recipe uses burnt sugar.

INGREDIENTS

Makes one 10-inch round cake

2 cups currants
3 cups raisins
1 cup prunes, pitted
⅔ cup mixed citrus peel
2¼ cups dark brown sugar
1 teaspoon ground cinnamon
6 tablespoons rum, plus more if needed
1¼ cups sherry, plus more if needed
1 pound/2 cups softened butter
10 eggs, beaten
1 pound/4 cups self-rising flour
1 teaspoon vanilla extract

1 Wash the currants, raisins, prunes and mixed peel, then pat dry. Place in a food processor and process until finely chopped. Transfer to a large, clean jar or bowl, add ¾ cup of the sugar, the mixed spice, rum and sherry. Mix very well and then cover with a lid and set aside for anything from 2 weeks to 3 months – the longer it is left, the better the flavor will be.

2 Stir the fruit mixture occasionally and keep covered, adding more rum and sherry, if you like.

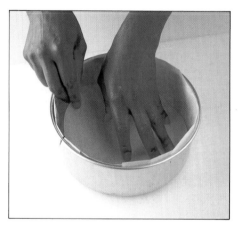

3 Preheat the oven to 325°F. Grease and line a 10-inch round cake pan with a double layer of wax paper.

4 Sift the flour, and set aside. Cream together the butter and remaining sugar and beat in the eggs until the mixture is smooth and creamy.

5 Add the fruit mixture, then gradually stir in the flour and vanilla extract. Mix well, adding 1–2 tablespoons sherry if the mixture is too stiff; it should just fall off the back of the spoon, but should not be too runny.

6 Spoon the mixture into the prepared pan, cover loosely with foil and bake for about 2½ hours until the cake is firm and springy. Leave to cool in the pan overnight, then sprinkle with more rum if the cake is not to be used immediately. Wrap the cake in foil to keep it moist.

--- COOK'S TIP ---

Although the dried fruits are chopped in a food processor, they can be marinated whole, if preferred. If you don't have enough time to marinate the fruit, simmer the fruit in the liquor mixture for about 30 minutes, and leave overnight.

SPICED DRINKS

Spices are added to a wide range of drinks and Sangrita, from Mexico, even uses fresh green chilies! Cocktails such as Bloody Maria are pepped up with Worcestershire and Tabasco sauces, while Caribbean punches, including Caribbean Cream Stout Punch, are enlivened with a sprinkling of spice. Mulled Wine and Spiced Mocha Drink are hot favorites too.

Spiced Mocha Drink

This spicy chocolate milk drink can be served either hot or cold – depending on the weather and your preference.

INGREDIENTS

Serves 4

6 ounces milk chocolate
½ cup light cream
3 cups hot black coffee
½ teaspoon ground cinnamon
whipped cream or ice, to serve

1 Using a sharp knife, cut the chocolate into small pieces to enable it to melt quickly and evenly.

2 Put the chocolate into a double saucepan or a bowl set over a saucepan of almost simmering water. The bottom of the bowl should not touch the water.

3 Add the light cream to the melting chocolate in the bowl, then stir well to mix.

4 Continue to heat gently until the chocolate is melted and smooth, stirring occasionally. Remove the bowl from the heat.

5 Add the coffee and cinnamon to the chocolate and whisk until foamy. Divide between four serving glasses, then either serve hot with a spoonful of cream, or cool and chill, and serve over ice.

COOK'S TIP

If any steam gets into the chocolate while you are melting it, it may turn into a solid mass. If this should happen, stir in about 1 teaspoon butter or margarine for each 1 ounce of chocolate.

Mulled Wine

Cloves, cinnamon and nutmeg are used to flavor this spicy mulled wine. It makes an ideal drink for a party in the winter and it is bound to warm everybody up.

INGREDIENTS

Makes 16 x ²/₃ cup glasses

1 orange
4 tablespoons raw sugar
grated nutmeg
2 cinnamon sticks
few cloves, plus extra for studding
2 tablespoons seedless raisins
5 tablespoons honey
2 clementines
6¼ cups inexpensive claret
2½ cups medium cider
1¼ cups orange juice

──── VARIATION ────

Vary the spices used in this mulled wine – whole allspice can be added instead of cinnamon sticks. If you like, you can also add a selection of sliced citrus fruits.

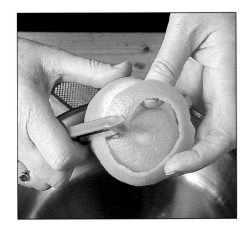

1 With a sharp knife or a rotary peeler, pare off a long strip of orange peel.

2 Place the sugar, nutmeg, cinnamon, cloves, raisins, honey and peel in a large saucepan. Stud the clementines with cloves and add them to the pan. Add the claret and heat gently until the sugar has dissolved. Pour in the cider and continue to gently heat the mulled wine. Do not boil.

3 Add the orange juice to the pan and warm through. Remove the clementines and cinnamon sticks and strain the mulled wine into a warmed punch bowl or other serving bowl. Add the clove-studded clementines and serve hot in warmed glasses, or in glasses containing a small spoon (to prevent the glass breaking).

Sangrita

INGREDIENTS

Serves 8
1 pound tomatoes, peeled, seeded
   and chopped
½ cup orange juice
4 tablespoons freshly squeezed
   lime juice
1 small onion, chopped
½ teaspoon granulated sugar
6 small fresh green chilies, seeded
   and chopped
Aged tequila (*Tequila Añejo*)
salt

> ── COOK'S TIP ──
>
> Plain white tequila is not suitable for this drink. Choose one of the amber aged tequilas (*añejos*), which are smoother and gentler on the palate.

1 Put the tomatoes, orange juice, lime juice, onion, sugar and green chilies in a food processor.

2 Process the tomato mixture until very smooth, scraping down the sides if necessary.

3 Pour the tomato mixture into a pitcher and chill well.

4 Pour into small glasses, allowing about 6 tablespoons per portion. Pour the tequila into small glasses, allowing 2 ounces per person. Sip the tomato juice and tequila alternately.

Sangria

This very popular summer drink was borrowed from Spain. The Mexican version is slightly lower in alcohol than the original.

INGREDIENTS

Serves 6
ice cubes
4 cups dry red table wine
⅔ cup freshly squeezed
   orange juice
¼ cup freshly squeezed
   lime juice
½ cup caster sugar
½ teaspoon ground cinnamon
2 limes or 1 apple, sliced, to serve

1 Half fill a large pitcher with ice cubes. Pour in the wine and the orange and lime juices.

2 Add the sugar and cinnamon and stir well until it has dissolved. Pour into tumblers and float the lime or apple slices on top. Serve at once.

> ── COOK'S TIP ──
>
> Sugar does not dissolve readily in alcohol. It is best to use simple syrup, which is very easy to make and gives a smoother drink. Combine 2 cups granulated sugar and 2 cups water in a pitcher and set aside until the sugar has dissolved. Stir from time to time. 1 tablespoon simple syrup is the equivalent of 1½ teaspoons sugar.

Bloody Maria

INGREDIENTS

Serves 2

³/₄ cup tomato juice
6 tablespoons white tequila
dash each Worcestershire and
    Tabasco sauces
2 tablespoons lemon juice
8 ice cubes
salt and freshly ground black pepper

COOK'S TIP

When drinks are to be served with ice,
make sure all the ingredients are thoroughly chilled ahead of time.

1 Combine the tomato juice, tequila,
    Worcestershire and Tabasco sauces,
and lemon juice in a cocktail shaker.
Add salt and pepper to taste, and four
ice cubes. Shake very vigorously.

2 Place the remaining ice cubes in
    two heavy-based glasses and strain
the tequila over them.

Margarita

Tequila is made from the sap of a
fleshy-leafed plant called the blue
agave and gets its name from the
town of Tequila, where it has
been made for more than 200
years. The Margarita is the most
well-known drink made with
tequila.

INGREDIENTS

Serves 2

½ lime or lemon
salt
½ cup white tequila
2 tablespoons Triple Sec or
    Cointreau
2 tablespoons freshly squeezed lime or
    lemon juice
4 or more ice cubes

COOK'S TIP

It really is worth going to the trouble of
buying limes for this recipe. Lemons will
do, but something of the special flavor of
the drink will be lost in the substitution.

1 Rub the rims of two cocktail
    glasses with the lime. Pour some
salt into a saucer and dip in the glass
rims so that they are frosted.

2 Combine the tequila, Triple Sec,
    and lime juice in a pitcher and stir
to mix well.

3 Pour the tequila mixture into the
    prepared glasses. Add the ice cubes
and serve at once.

Demerara Rum Punch

The inspiration for this punch came from the rum distillery at Plantation Diamond Estate in Guyana where some of the finest rum in the world is made, and the tantalizing aromas of sugar cane and rum pervade the air.

INGREDIENTS

Serves 4
⅔ cup orange juice
⅔ cup pineapple juice
⅔ cup mango juice
½ cup water
1 cup dark rum
a shake of Angostura bitters
freshly grated nutmeg
2 tablespoons raw sugar
1 small banana
1 large orange

1 Pour the orange, pineapple and mango juices into a large punch bowl. Stir in the water.

2 Add the rum, Angostura bitters, nutmeg and sugar. Stir gently for a few minutes until the sugar has dissolved.

3 Slice the banana and stir gently into the punch.

4 Slice the orange and add to the punch. Chill and serve with ice.

COOK'S TIP

You can use white rum instead of dark, if you prefer. To make a stronger punch, add more rum.

Caribbean Cream Stout Punch

A well-known "pick-me-up" that is popular all over the Caribbean.

INGREDIENTS

Serves 2

2 cups stout
1¼ cups evaporated milk
5 tablespoons condensed milk
5 tablespoons sherry
2 or 3 drops vanilla extract
freshly grated nutmeg

1 Mix together the stout, evaporated and condensed milks, sherry and vanilla extract in a blender or food processor, or whisk together in a large mixing bowl, until creamy.

2 Add a little grated nutmeg to the stout mixture and blend or whisk again for a few minutes.

3 Chill for at least 45 minutes or until really cold before serving.

Index

almonds: cinnamon balls, 235
  spicy vegetables with
    almonds, 164
apple and cinnamon crumble
  cake, 236
apricot chutney, 210
avocados: avocado salad in ginger
    and orange sauce, 225
  guacamole, 48

baklava, 230
Balti potatoes, 162
bamie goreng, 189
bananas: banana ginger cake, 238
  spiced nutty bananas, 227
barbecued jerk chicken, 122
barbecued pork spareribs, 98
basmati and nut pilaf, 183
bass: Mexican spicy fish, 76
beancurd: curry fried noodles, 194
  Szechuan spicy beancurd, 134
beansprouts: vegetarian fried
    noodles, 198
beef: beef and eggplant
    curry, 117
  beef and turmeric soup, 24
  beef enchiladas, 102
  beef with cactus pieces, 100
  French beans, rice and
    beef, 187
  spicy kebabs, 58
  spicy meat-filled
    packages, 54
  spicy meat fritters, 98
  spicy meatballs, 116
  Szechuan spicy beancurd, 134
  Tex-Mex baked potatoes with
    chili, 101
berry salsa, 208
black bean burritos, 139
black-eyed pea stew with spicy
    pumpkin, 152
blackened hot chicken breasts, 123
bloody Maria, 250
bon-bon chicken with spicy
    sesame, 127
bread pudding, spiced, 231
broccoli, penne with chili
    and, 196
burritos, black bean, 139
butterflied shrimp in chili
    chocolate, 38

cabbage: coleslaw in triple-hot
    dressing, 148
  spicy cabbage, 146
  vinegared chili cabbage, 148
cactus pieces, beef with, 100
Cajun "popcorn", 43
cakes: apple and cinnamon
    crumble cake, 236
  banana ginger cake, 238
  Caribbean fruit and rum
    cake, 242
  peach kuchen, 241
  spiced date and walnut
    cake, 239

caramel rice pudding, 232
Caribbean cream stout punch, 253
Caribbean fruit and rum cake, 242
Caribbean lamb curry, 105
Caribbean spiced fish, 85
carrots: spiced carrot dip, 220
  spicy carrots, 142
catfish: fried catfish fillets with
    piquant sauce, 67
cauliflower: fava bean and
    cauliflower curry, 145
chayotes: shrimp with chayote in
    turmeric sauce, 70
cheese: chili bean dip, 218
  desert nachos, 52
  quesadillas, 44
  red rice rissoles, 176
  tasty toasts, 210
  Welsh rabbit, 55
cheese, soft: cheese fritters, 62
  spicy noodle dessert, 224
chick-peas: hummus, 40
chicken: bamie goreng, 189
  barbecued jerk chicken, 122
  blackened hot chicken
    breasts, 123
  bon-bon chicken with spicy
    sesame, 127
  chicken jambalaya, 174
  chicken mulligatawny, 34
  chicken naan pockets, 56
  chicken sauce piquante, 128
  chicken tikka, 56
  curried noodle and chicken
    soup, 35
  ginger, chicken and coconut
    soup, 28
  hot chicken curry, 124
  mulligatawny soup, 25
  nasi goreng, 173
  San Francisco chicken
    wings, 42
  spicy chicken with
    coconut, 119
  spicy fried chicken, 118
  spicy masala chicken, 131
  spicy rice with chicken, 184
  spicy Szechuan noodles, 200
  tandoori chicken, 130
  yogurt chicken and rice, 168
chiles rellenos, 154
chili, red bean, 153
chilies: chili bean dip, 218
  chili crabs, 84
  chili relish, 219
  chili zucchini, 140
  citrus fish with
    chilies, 77
  double chili salsa, 212
  fiery citrus salsa, 206
  fried dough balls with fiery
    salsa, 60
  fried fish in green chili
    sauce, 82
  green bean and chili pepper
    salad, 157
  green chili dhal, 136

jalapeño and shrimp salad, 158
lamb stew, 106
Mexican-style rice, 191
mole poblano de
    Guajolote, 114
mushrooms with chipotle
    chilies, 158
penne with chili and
    broccoli, 196
pork with chilies and
    pineapple, 113
potatoes with red chilies, 135
salt cod in mild chili sauce, 73
sangrita, 248
steamed fish with chili
    sauce, 66
stir-fried chili greens, 156
tasty toasts, 210
Tex-Mex baked potatoes with
    chili, 101
vegetables in peanut and chili
    sauce, 150
vinegar chili fish, 74
vinegared chili cabbage, 148
chocolate: spiced mocha
    drink, 246
chutney, apricot, 210
cinnamon balls, 235
cinnamon rolls, 240
citrus fish with chilies, 77
coconut: coconut and peanut
    relish, 204
  coconut chili relish, 216
coconut milk:
  coconut and nutmeg ice
    cream, 229
  coconut rice, 184
  curried shrimp in coconut
    milk, 94
  festive rice, 179
  ginger, chicken and coconut
    soup, 28
  jumbo shrimp in spiced
    coconut sauce, 88
  spicy chicken with coconut, 119
cod: Caribbean spiced fish, 85
  cod with chili and mustard
    seeds, 59
  seafood and rice, 174
  spicy fish and rice, 170
  see also salt cod
coffee: spiced mocha drink, 246
coleslaw in triple-hot dressing, 148
coriander rice, 106
corn: plantain soup with corn and
    chili, 22
cornmeal, spicy shrimp with, 93
crabs, chili, 84
crayfish: Cajun "popcorn", 43
cucumbers, pickled, 214
curries: beef and eggplant
    curry, 117
  Caribbean lamb curry, 105
  curried noodle and chicken
    soup, 35
  curried shrimp and saltfish, 88
  curried shrimp in coconut

milk, 94
curry fried noodles, 194
fava bean and cauliflower
    curry, 145
hot chicken curry, 124
jumbo shrimp in curry
    sauce, 82
khara masala lamb, 110
pineapple curry with prawns
    and mussels, 94
yellow curry paste, 94

daikon, 62
dates: date and nut pastries, 234
  spiced date and walnut
    cake, 239
demerara rum punch, 252
desert nachos, 52
deviled kidneys, 51
dips: chili bean dip, 218
  guacamole, 48
  hummus, 40
  spiced carrot dip, 220
dough balls, fried with fiery
    salsa, 60
dried fruit: Caribbean fruit and
    rum cake, 242
drinks, 244-53
duck, crispy and aromatic, 120
dumplins, spicy fried, 215

eggplant: beef and eggplant
    curry, 117
eggs: huevos rancheros, 52
  stir-fried chili greens, 156
  tomato noodles with fried
    egg, 194
enchiladas: beef enchiladas, 102
  red enchiladas, 104

falafel, 40
fava beans: fava bean and
    cauliflower curry, 145
  fava beans in hot sauce, 144
fenugreek, masala beans with, 165
festive rice, 179
fish and seafood, 64-95
  baked or grilled spiced whole
    fish, 74
  braised fish in chili and garlic
    sauce, 72
  pickled fish, 68
  steamed fish with chili
    sauce, 66
  see also individual types of fish
frijoles, 138
  refried beans (frijoles
    refritos), 140
fritters: cheese, 62
  spicy meat, 98
fruit: berry salsa, 208
  caramel rice pudding, 232
  see also individual types of fruit
fruit salads: avocado salad in ginger
    and orange sauce, 225
  fruits of the tropics salad, 228

ginger: avocado salad in ginger and orange sauce, 225
    banana ginger cake, 238
    fresh pineapple with ginger, 226
    ginger, chicken and coconut soup, 28
green beans: green bean and chili pepper salad, 157
    green beans, rice and beef, 187
    masala beans with fenugreek, 165
groundnut soup, spicy, 22
guacamole, 48

halibut: citrus fish with chilies, 77
hot and sour shrimp soup with lemon grass, 28
huevos rancheros, 52
hummus, 40

ice cream, coconut and nutmeg, 229
Indian pilau rice, 180
Indonesian spicy fish, 70

jalapeño and shrimp salad, 158
jerk chicken, barbecued, 122

kachumbali salad, 216
kebabs: marinated vegetables on skewers, 151
    spiced fish kebabs, 86
    spicy kebabs, 58
Kenyan mung bean stew, 143
khara masala lamb, 110
kidney beans see red kidney beans
kidneys, deviled, 51

lamb: Caribbean lamb curry, 105
    khara masala lamb, 110
    lamb stew, 106
    lamb tagine with cilantro and spices, 109
    spiced lamb soup, 30
lemon grass shrimp on crisp noodle cake, 90
lentils: green chili dhal, 136
    okra with green mango and lentils, 162
    Persian rice with a tahdeeg, 178
Louisiana rice, 169

mackerel: Indonesian spicy fish, 70
    vinegar chili fish, 74
mangoes: okra with green mango and lentils, 162
margarita, 250
marinated vegetables on skewers, 151
masala beans with fenugreek, 165
masala mashed potatoes, 146
masala shrimp and rice, 170
meat and poultry, 96-131
    see also individual types of meat
meatballs, spicy, 116
Mexican spicy fish, 76
Mexican-style rice, 191

mocha drink, spiced, 246
mole poblano de Guajolote, 114
monkfish packages, chilied, 46
mulled wine, 247
mulligatawny soup, 25
    chicken mulligatawny, 34
mung bean stew, Kenyan, 143
mushrooms with chipotle chilies, 158
mussels: pineapple curry with shrimp and mussels, 94
    tossed noodles with seafood, 192

naan pockets, chicken, 56
nachos, desert, 52
nasi goreng, 173
noodles: bamie goreng, 189
    chilled soba noodles with nori, 62
    crisp fried rice vermicelli, 197
    curried noodle and chicken soup, 35
    curry fried noodles, 194
    lemon grass shrimp on crisp noodle cake, 90
    noodle soup with pork and Szechuan pickle, 32
    noodles with spicy meat sauce, 192
    sesame noodles with scallions, 200
    spicy noodle pudding, 224
    spicy Szechuan noodles, 200
    Thai fried noodles, 199
    tomato noodles with fried egg, 194
    tossed noodles with seafood, 192
    vegetarian fried noodles, 198
nori: chilled soba noodles with nori, 62
    sushi, 186
nuts: basmati and nut pilaf, 183
    date and nut pastries, 234
    spiced nutty bananas, 227

oatmeal: banana ginger cake, 238
okra: okra fried rice, 180
    okra with green mango and lentils, 162
    spicy shrimp with okra, 92
onions: kachumbali salad, 216
    red onion raita, 221
    tomato and onion salad, 204
orange: avocado salad in ginger and orange sauce, 225
    fiery citrus salsa, 206

pastries: baklava, 230
    cinnamon rolls, 240
    date and nut pastries, 234
    samosas, 47
    spicy meat-filled parcels, 54
peach kuchen, 241
peanut butter: spicy groundnut soup, 22

vegetables in peanut and chili sauce, 150
peanuts: coconut and peanut relish, 204
peas: Mexican-style rice, 191
penne with chili and broccoli, 196
pepper soup, spicy, 31
peppers: chiles rellenos, 154
    green bean and chili pepper salad, 157
    peppery bean salad, 161
Persian rice with a tahdeeg, 178
pickled fish, 68
pickles: mixed vegetable pickle, 209
    pickled cucumbers, 214
pilaf: basmati and nut, 183
    pistachio, 182
    spiced trout, 172
pilau rice, Indian, 180
pineapple: fresh pineapple with ginger, 226
    pineapple curry with shrimp and mussels, 94
    piquant pineapple relish, 213
    pork with chilies and pineapple, 113
pistachio nuts: baklava, 230
    pistachio pilaf, 182
plantain soup with corn and chili, 22
pomfret: fried fish in green chili sauce, 82
pork: barbecued pork spareribs, 98
    deep-fried spareribs with spicy salt and pepper, 112
    Louisiana rice, 169
    nasi goreng, 173
    noodle soup with pork and Szechuan pickle, 32
    noodles with spicy meat sauce, 192
    pork with chilies and pineapple, 113
    sweet and sour pork, 108
potatoes: Balti potatoes, 162
    masala mashed potatoes, 146
    potatoes with red chilies, 135
    spicy potato salad, 160
    spicy potatoes, 39
    Tex-Mex baked potatoes with chili, 101
poultry and meat, 96-131
poussins, spatchcocked deviled, 126
pumpkin: black-eyed pea stew with spicy pumpkin, 152
    pumpkin and chili soup, 20
punch: Caribbean cream stout punch, 253
    demerara rum punch, 252

quail's eggs: stir-fried chili greens, 156
quesadillas, 44

raita, red onion, 221
red kidney beans: chili bean dip, 218
    frijoles, 138
    peppery bean salad, 161
    red bean chili, 153
    Tex-Mex baked potatoes with chili, 101
red mullet: Turkish cold fish, 81
red snapper: red snapper, Veracruz-style, 69
    snapper, tomato and tamarind noodle soup, 32
    whole fish with sweet and sour sauce, 80
refried beans (frijoles refritos), 140
    huevos rancheros, 52
relishes: chili, 219
    coconut and peanut, 204
    coconut chili, 216
    kachumbali salad, 216
    piquant pineapple, 213
rice: basmati and nut pilaf, 183
    caramel rice pudding, 232
    chicken jambalaya, 174
    coconut rice, 184
    festive rice, 179
    green beans, rice and beef, 187
    Indian pilau rice, 180
    Louisiana rice, 169
    masala shrimp and rice, 170
    Mexican-style rice, 191
    nasi goreng, 173
    okra fried rice, 180
    Persian rice with a tahdeeg, 178
    pistachio pilaf, 182
    red rice rissoles, 176
    rice with dill and spicy beans, 190
    seafood and rice, 174
    spiced rice pudding, 232
    spiced trout pilaf, 172
    spicy fish and rice, 170
    spicy rice cakes, 176
    spicy rice with chicken, 184
    sushi, 186
    sweet and sour rice, 188
    yogurt chicken and rice, 168
rissoles, red rice, 176
rolls, cinnamon, 240
rum punch, demerara, 252

saffron fish, 78
salads: green bean and chili pepper, 157
    jalapeño and shrimp, 158
    peppery bean, 161
    spicy potato, 160
    tomato and onion, 204
    see also fruit salads
salmon: sushi, 186
salmon trout: saffron fish, 78
salsa: berry salsa, 208
    double chili salsa, 212
    fiery citrus salsa, 206
    fried dough balls with fiery salsa, 60

salsa verde, 207
tomato salsa, 48
salt cod in mild chili sauce, 73
saltfish, curried shrimp and, 88
samosas, 47
San Francisco chicken wings, 42
sangria, 248
sangrita, 248
sardines, pan-fried spicy, 78
scallions, sesame noodles with, 200
seafood and fish, 64-95
    hot and spicy seafood soup, 27
    seafood and rice, 174
    seafood wontons with spicy
        dressing, 50
    tossed noodles with
        seafood, 192
seaweed: chilled soba noodles with
    nori, 62
    sushi, 186
sesame noodles with scallions, 200
shrimp: butterflied shrimp in chili
    chocolate, 38
    Cajun "popcorn", 43
    curried shrimp and saltfish, 88
    curried shrimp in coconut
        milk, 94
    hot and sour shrimp soup with
        lemon grass, 28
    jalapeño and shrimp salad, 158
    jumbo shrimp in curry sauce, 82
    lemon grass shrimp on crisp
        noodle cake, 90
    masala shrimp and rice, 170
    pineapple curry with shrimp
        and mussels, 94
    seafood and rice, 174
    seafood wontons with spicy
        dressing, 50
    shrimp in spiced coconut
        sauce, 88
    shrimp in spicy tomato
        sauce, 86
    shrimp with chayote in
        turmeric sauce, 70
    spicy shrimp with cornmeal, 93
    spicy shrimp with okra, 92
    stir-fried shrimp with
        tamarind, 91
    tossed noodles with
        seafood, 192
shrimp paste, 20, 27
smoked trout: spiced trout
    pilaf, 172
soups, 16-35
    beef and turmeric, 24
    chicken mulligatawny, 34
    curried noodle and
        chicken, 35
    ginger, chicken and
        coconut, 28
    hot and sour shrimp with
        lemon grass, 28
    hot and spicy seafood, 27
    mulligatawny, 25
    noodle soup with pork and
        Szechuan pickle, 32

plantain with corn and
    chili, 22
pumpkin and chili, 20
snapper, tomato and tamarind
    noodle, 32
spiced lamb, 30
spicy groundnut, 22
spicy pepper, 31
spicy vegetable, 21
spicy yogurt, 26
tamarind with peanuts and
    vegetables, 19
tortilla, 18
spareribs see pork
spatchcocked deviled
    poussins, 126
spicy fried dumplins, 215
spicy potatoes, 39
spinach: stir-fried chili greens, 156
squid: tossed noodles with
    seafood, 192
stout punch, Caribbean cream, 253
sushi, 186
sweet and sour pork, 108
sweet and sour rice, 188
sweet and sour sauce, whole fish
    with, 80
swordfish: spiced fish
    kebabs, 86
Szechuan spicy beancurd, 134

tagine, lamb, 109
tamarind: stir-fried shrimp with
    tamarind, 91
    tamarind soup with peanuts and
        vegetables, 19
tandoori chicken, 130
tequila: bloody Maria, 250
    margarita, 250
Tex-Mex baked potatoes with
    chili, 101
Thai fried noodles, 199
toasts, tasty, 210
tomatoes: bloody Maria, 250
    kachumbali salad, 216
    Mexican-style rice, 191
    red snapper, Veracruz-style, 69
    sangrita, 248
    shrimp in spicy tomato
        sauce, 86
    snapper, tomato and tamarind
        noodle soup, 32
    tomato and onion salad, 204
    tomato noodles with fried
        egg, 194
    tomato salsa, 48
tortilla chips: desert nachos, 52
tortillas: beef enchiladas, 102
    black bean burritos, 139
    huevos rancheros, 52
    mixed tostadas, 44
    quesadillas, 44
    red enchiladas, 104
    tortilla soup, 18
tostadas, mixed, 44
trout, smoked see smoked trout
tuna: sushi, 186

turkey: mole poblano de
    Guajolote, 114
Turkish cold fish, 81

vegetables, 132-65
    marinated vegetables on
        skewers, 151
    mixed vegetable pickle, 209
    spicy vegetable soup, 21
    spicy vegetables with
        almonds, 164
    tamarind soup with peanuts and
        vegetables, 19
    vegetables in peanut and chili
        sauce, 150
    see also individual types of
        vegetable
vegetarian fried noodles, 198
vermicelli: crisp fried rice
    vermicelli, 197
vinegar chili fish, 74
vinegared chili cabbage, 148

walnuts: spiced date and walnut
    cake, 239
Welsh rabbit, 55
white beans: falafel, 40
wine: mulled wine, 247
    sangria, 248
wontons: seafood wontons with
    spicy dressing, 50

yogurt: spicy yogurt soup, 26
    yogurt chicken and rice, 168

zereshk, 188
zucchini, chili, 140